CEREMONIES OF THE LITURGICAL YEAR

PETER J. ELLIOTT

Ceremonies of the Liturgical Year

According to the Modern Roman Rite

A Manual for Clergy and All
Involved in Liturgical Ministries

IGNATIUS PRESS   SAN FRANCISCO

Nihil Obstat: Very Reverend Peter J. Kenny, D.D.
Diocesan Censor
Archdiocese of Melbourne

Imprimatur: Reverend Msgr. Christopher Prowse, B.A.,
B. Theol., S.T.L., S.T.D.
Vicar General
Archdiocese of Melbourne

January 21, 2002

The English translation of the Table of Liturgical Days according to Their Order of Preference in the "General Norms for the Liturgical Year and the Calendar" from *Documents on the Liturgy, 1963–1979: Conciliar, Papal, and Curial Texts* © 1982, International Committee on English in the Liturgy, Inc. All rights reserved. (Adapted to reflect changes in the Missale Romanum, 2002.)

Proclamation of the Birth of Christ, Proclamation of the Date of Easter on Epiphany, and the *Reception of the Holy Oils Blessed at the Chrism Mass* © 1994 United States Conference of Catholic Bishops, Inc., Washington, D.C. Reprinted with permission. All rights reserved.

Cover design by Roxanne Mei Lum

© 2002 Ignatius Press, San Francisco
All rights reserved
ISBN 978-0-89870-829-5 (PB)
ISBN 978-1-68149-082-3 (eBook)
Library of Congress Control number 2001094793
Printed in the United States of America ∞

Pro peregrinatoribus

Contents

CONTENTS

Foreword

The liturgy of the Catholic Church is the action by which Jesus Christ unites the members of the Church in glorifying God. It makes people holy through words, music, action and signs.

What we do as we celebrate the Eucharist, the sacraments and sacramentals is intended to be the most powerful means of union with our God, with the saints in heaven and with each other, and is to be a foretaste of the praise of God given in joy and peace by the saints in heaven.

As we move through the whole of the year, the Church is united with the mysteries of Christ's earthly life so as to come closer with love as a priestly people to her Lord and Saviour.

Monsignor Peter Elliott provides scholarship and many years' experience of and love of the liturgy in *Ceremonies of the Liturgical Year*. His previous work *Ceremonies of the Modern Roman Rite* has helped many people to celebrate the liturgy with attention and devotion. He has also achieved wide experience in the Archdiocese of Melbourne as a priest, as an author of many books, and as an official of the Pontifical Council for the Family in the Vatican. For the last four years he has been Episcopal Vicar for Religious Education in the Archdiocese of Melbourne and has led the publication of *To Know, Worship and Love*, the religious education texts for the whole of primary and secondary schooling.

Monsignor Elliott has provided the present work as a guide to the most important moments of the Church year from Advent and Christmas to Holy Week, Corpus Christi and to the Solemnity of Christ the King. His book also has been a long-awaited guide to those who wish to celebrate the events of the Church year with dignity, devotion and deep faith. The Church of Melbourne is deeply grateful to Monsignor Elliott for this book, which will be widely welcomed throughout the English-speaking world.

May it be a fitting instrument to guide the Church in proclaiming and celebrating the mystery of Christ in her liturgy, so that the faithful may live from it and bear witness to it in the world.

+ Denis J. Hart
Archbishop of Melbourne

November 1, 2002
Solemnity of All Saints

Preface

This work is a sequel to *Ceremonies of the Modern Roman Rite*, a guide to the ceremonial of the Eucharist and the Liturgy of the Hours, published by Ignatius Press in 1995. A Spanish translation of this book was published in 1996 under the title *Guia pratica de liturgia*, by Ediciones Universidad de Navarra, Pamplona.

In *Ceremonies of the Liturgical Year*, I offer detailed guidance to the ceremonial of the rites proposed in the Missal and other authoritative books to be celebrated on the principal solemnities and feasts and during the seasons of the Roman Calendar. This work should be used in conjunction with *Ceremonies of the Modern Roman Rite*. It presupposes the celebration of the Mass presented in that book and is cross-referenced accordingly. It is in accord with the revised *General Instruction of the Roman Missal* (2002) prepared for the third edition of the *Missale Romanum*. In a further volume in this series I hope to present the ceremonies of the sacraments and funerals.

In the first place, I thank the Most Rev. Denis J. Hart, Archbishop of Melbourne for all his patient assistance. Advice and assistance were also given by the Most Rev. Geoffrey Jarrett, Bishop of Lismore; Rev. Msgr. James O'Brien; Rev. David Cartwright; Rev. Charles Portelli; Rev. Gregory Pritchard, Rev. Anthony Robbie, Dom Alcuin Reid, O.S.B., and Rev. Joseph Illo. In no way are they bound to the opinions and interpretations in this book.

In describing the ceremonies of Holy Week, I was inspired by the Venerable English College, Rome, as I have assisted at these celebrations there while working in the

Roman Curia. I thank the Rector at that time, Msgr. Adrian Toffolo, and the staff and students for the experience of noble liturgy, at once ordered, prayerful and pastoral.

Finally, I express my gratitude to the dedicated staff of Ignatius Press. Their interest and advice have once again been most encouraging.

— Rev. Msgr. Peter J. Elliott, E.V.
Melbourne 2002

Abbreviations

CB	*Ceremonial of Bishops*
CCC	*Catechism of the Catholic Church*
CIC	*Codex Iuris Canonici, Code of Canon Law*
CLE	*Circular Letter concerning the Preparation and Celebration of the Easter Feasts*
CMRR	*Ceremonies of the Modern Roman Rite*
GIRM	*General Instruction of the Roman Missal* (revised 2002)
LY	*General Norms for the Liturgical Year and the Calendar* (Roman Missal)
MR	*Missale Romanum, Roman Missal*
PR	*Pontificale Romanum, Roman Pontifical*
RR	*Rituale Romanum, Roman Ritual*
SC	Vatican II, *Sacrosanctum Concilium, The Constitution on the Sacred Liturgy*

Introduction

1. Christians understand time differently from other people because of the liturgical year. We are drawn into a cycle that can become such a part of our lives that it determines how we understand the structure of each passing year. In the mind of the Christian, each passing year takes shape, not so much around the cycle of natural seasons, the financial or sporting year or academic semesters, but around the feasts, fasts and seasons of the Catholic Church. Without thinking much about it, from early childhood, we gradually learn to see time itself, past, present and future, in a new way.

2. All of the great moments of the liturgical year look back to the salvific events of Jesus Christ, the Lord of history. Those events are made present here and now as offers of grace, yet they bear strong presentiments of eternity. Based on a common human consciousness of past, present and future, awareness of *sacred* time surely marks one of the profound differences between a Christian and a secularized person today. Before reflecting on the past, present and future dimensions of the liturgical year, it is important to understand the challenge we face in a secularized society.

Resacralizing Time

3. *Sacred time* is an instrument for catechesis and evangelization. The missionary monks who evangelized northern Europe knew that well when they transformed and adapted the existing pagan time cycles. For example, they noted how the natural season of spring coincided with the Christian

season of catechesis and penance leading to Easter, with the result that it became known among Anglo Saxon people simply as "Lenthen", "Spring". This is the source of our English word "Lent", rather than the expression "Forty Days" (Quadragesima) that is still used around the Mediterranean. Lent is a spiritual springtime of growth and new life. Another example is the way the date of Christ's birth replaced the pagan celebration of the winter solstice, celebrated on December 25 in ancient Rome. Time itself was "baptized" as new peoples entered the Church.

4. We face a rather different challenge in the third Christian millennium. We need to resacralize time in a secularized society that has abandoned our way of looking at the passing year. This surely challenges us to make the most of the powerful cycle of Christian feasts, fasts and seasons in the life of diocese, parish or religious community and family, above all in the reverent celebration of the customary rites and ceremonies of the Roman Rite that mark out sacred times. These ceremonies are described in detail in this book in order to help those who celebrate them to make them better proclaim the saving mysteries of the Incarnation and Redemption to Christ's faithful. The more noble, evocative and vivid is the ceremonial of our seasonal liturgies, the more those liturgies draw people into the mystery of Christ. Holy Week is the supreme example.

5. There are many practical ways of achieving this end, such as: announcing the feasts and seasons well in advance, planning and preparing the ceremonies well, bringing the meaning of a day or season into preaching, catechesis and public prayer. As part of this work of resacralizing time, the visual signs and symbols of the seasons should be exploited more than ever. Yet one still enters churches where the environment for the liturgy remains neutral throughout the year.

There are no visible indications of where God's Pilgrim People are at *this* point in their journey through the Year of Grace. Look around the church. The bare altar suggests that this might be Good Friday, while a mountain of flowers, left over from a wedding, tells us that it could just as well be Easter Day. Even the celebration of the liturgy only faintly reflects the day or season, perhaps in the color of vestments, and the result is monotony. There is no place for monotony, however, in the rich texture of Christian life and worship.

6. We are carried forward and freed from the mundane through the mystery and splendor of Catholic worship. The secular year may be rather bland. Any variety it may have is derived from a few civil or national holidays or commercialized versions of religious celebrations, such as Christmas, or frankly commercial ventures, such as Mothers' Day. But the Christian year has its own inner vitality. It does not need to be propped up by civil celebrations. Where these are customarily observed with Christian rites, they cannot be allowed to intrude into the order of the liturgy of the Church; otherwise we can lose sight of the priority of sacred time.

7. The genius of the liturgical year is the way it reminds us that time was transformed when the Divine Word became flesh. In that mystery of the Incarnation we may perceive that, in a sense, the *Word became time*. To put it another way, in Christ time takes on a sacramental dimension. The liturgical year bears this sacramental quality of memorial, actuation and prophecy. Time becomes a re-enactment of Christ's saving events, his being born in our flesh, his dying and rising for us in that human flesh. Time thus becomes a pressing sign of salvation, the "day of the Lord", his ever-present "hour of salvation", the *kairos*. Time on earth then becomes our

pilgrimage through and beyond death towards the future Kingdom. The liturgical year is best understood both in its origins and current form in the way we experience time: in the light of the past, present and future.

Remembering the Past

8. To recall the past is a universal human experience. We naturally celebrate past events in our own lives, beginning with birthdays. In Christian families, we recall anniversaries of marriage, ordination, religious profession and death, and in some cultures the name days of children or adults. In the life of a city, nation or race great events are remembered and celebrated. This natural human focus on a "great event" was the cause and beginning of the development of the liturgical year. Just as the Passover in Egypt was the key to the Jewish calendar, so the Resurrection of Jesus of Nazareth, at the time of Passover probably in A.D. 29, was the cause and beginning of Christianity, Christians and the Church.

9. The Christian calendar found its origins in Israel and the Jewish seven-day week. The "seventh day", the Sabbath, sanctified the whole Jewish week, with Monday and Thursday as two associated days of fasting among devout Jews at the time of Christ. So the Pharisee could say, "I fast twice a week" (Luke 18:12).

10. In apostolic times, Christians replaced the Sabbath with Sunday, the first day of the week, when Jesus Christ rose from the dead (cf. 1 Corinthians 15:2; Acts 20:7; and "the day of the Lord" in Revelation 1:10), although some Christians still retained an observance of the Sabbath alongside Sunday. The early Christians also retained two days of fasting, Wednesday and Friday (cf. *The Didache*, 8). Later, in the West, Saturday became a fast day. The Christian celebration of the Eucharist on Sunday was often preceded by

vigils, in the night or at daybreak, a form of worship partly influenced by Jewish domestic or synagogue prayer. In daily synagogue prayer we find the roots of the Divine Office or Liturgy of the Hours.

11. However, the weekly Sunday remembrance of the saving event of Easter was soon accompanied by a more solemn annual recalling of the Resurrection. This was the new Passover of the new Israel, Easter Sunday. In preparation for Easter, the days of Holy Week recalled the events of Christ's Passion through prayer and preaching. By the fourth century, a variety of ceremonies and customs had developed to celebrate Holy Week. Through the recollections of the pilgrim lady Egeria, we are able to see how the "Great Week" was observed in Jerusalem at the end of the fourth century.

12. Easter is the "mother of all the Christian feasts", not only because it is the supreme celebration of the Lord, but also because it is regarded as the "Great Sunday", the original Christian holy day. Calculated in different ways so as to coincide with the Jewish Passover, the date of Easter became the subject of a fierce and divisive debate among Christians. The first round was fought between Asian Christians and the other Churches in the second and third centuries. Later, when Roman and Celtic Christians came together, they faced the same differences, and the debate was taken up again. We find it difficult to understand the rancor and intensity of these early Christian arguments about sacred time. Saint Paul had already rejected a scrupulous preoccupation with the subtleties of the Jewish religious calendar (cf. Galatians 4:10, 11; Colossians 2:16), but this was something quite different.

13. For our forebears in the faith, it was very important to get the memories *right*. This was part of a conserving mentality

that sought to hand on and keep the apostolic tradition in its pristine purity. This applied whether Christians wanted to retain continuity with some elements in the Jewish calendar, such as the Passover and Pentecost, or whether they sought to distance themselves from Judaism, as in Syria. The second-century debates over the correct date of Easter reflect some of that tension, but more importantly they bear witness to the innate conservatism of early Christians.

14. The predominant practice was to celebrate Easter on the Sunday following the first full moon of springtime. But this collided with a minority tradition in Asia Minor, allegedly derived from Saint John. Here Easter was celebrated on the fourteenth day of the first full moon of springtime, the fourteenth of Nisan. Putting aside the arguments of either party, that the issue was taken so seriously tells us much of the mind of Christians in the imperial Roman age. Choosing the "right" times to celebrate or fast was important to our forebears in the faith. They regarded the calendar itself as a way of holding onto and passing on the apostolic tradition. Sacred time offered them a kind of "orthopraxis" that sustained their orthodoxy.

15. This distant debate reminds us that we may fail to appreciate the power and precision of *memory* in the ancient world. This failure is only too evident in those scriptural critics who are sceptical about the historical roots of our faith, above all the historicity of events recorded in the Gospels. But ours is a historical religion, and the historical basis of Christianity is reflected in the early developments of the sacred calendar that became our liturgical year. The first Christians knew what some of us tend to forget, that Christianity stands or falls on the reality of specific events that occurred in the first century. Close to those events, influenced by disciples of the first witnesses, they passed on those unique reve-

latory moments within the community of the Church, not only in Scripture and tradition, in doctrines and sacraments, but in the way they celebrated times and seasons. Through the temporal cycle they relived and proclaimed the saving events of the Lord.

16. *Anamnesis*, memorial, is the Jewish principle behind this Christian celebration of time, derived as it is in part from the calendar of Israel. Memorial has been developed well in the *Catechism of the Catholic Church* (1362–72), that is, in terms of the "great memorial" of the Holy Eucharist. What is remembered is not merely celebrated, but relived or made present again, re-presented or re-played. This is a key to Catholic teaching on how the Eucharistic Sacrifice is the re-presentation of the Paschal Mystery, the Cross and Resurrection. But it also shows us how our liturgical year is much more than a series of anniversaries.

17. Through *anamnesis*, the passing days and months become the Year of Grace. Events that happened in time are now extended in sacrifice and sacrament throughout one recurring year of our time. The prescribed ceremonies for Holy Week and the Easter Triduum, especially the Easter Vigil, are the clearest examples of *anamnesis* focused on the solemn rites of Christian Initiation and the Eucharist. The timing and process of preparing people for sacramental incorporation into the Church was determined in part by the celebration of Easter, regarded as the right moment to incorporate converts into the saving grace of the risen Christ. But the catechumenate also partly influenced the development of the calendar, as a Lenten fast for all believers took shape as well as the catechumenal Advent that emerged in Gaul. The catechumens were brought into the memory of the Church through observing the sacred times of the community of faith. Conversion meant entering a new structure of time.

18.   By the late fourth century, the basic shape of our liturgical year was well established. The birth of Christ was celebrated on December 25 in the West and January 6 in the East, although the precise origins of these dates remain a matter for academic speculation. A Lenten fast was observed, varying in length and intensity from place to place. Holy Week or Great Week was a time of prayer and fasting leading to the supreme celebration, Easter Day, which was extended to the fifty days of Easter culminating with the feast of Pentecost, the outpouring of the Holy Spirit. Within a relatively short time the season of Advent was added to this basic calendar in Rome. Days of fasting, such as the Ember Days, days associated with a papal Mass celebrated at specific stational churches, vigils, and octaves gradually entered the Roman calendar as ways for the faithful to prepare for or extend the celebration of great feasts. But the whole annual cycle encapsulated salvation history. Through festival and fast, believers could relive and enter the events of the Savior, celebrated and made present in the liturgy and sacraments.

19.   The cycle of saints' days represents a second level of this form of *anamnesis*. It would be wrong to imagine that saints' days were later medieval additions to a primitive Easter-centered liturgical year. Keeping careful record of the days when martyrs died and celebrating these anniversaries goes back to the second century. Well before the imperial persecutions ceased, in East and West there were lists of the anniversaries of the martyrs, the basic martyrologies. This early development also set up the distinction that continues to our times between universal or regional calendars and local calendars. The memory of the Universal Church includes the memories of particular Churches gathered in one communion. The calendars embrace all the saints and heroes of the Church who now share in the eternal Easter that we can enter through *anamnesis*.

The Present Offer of Grace

20. The "Year of Grace" reflects the *kairos* of the Lord, his "chosen time". The *kairos* is God's ever-present offer of grace to us in chosen moments of time, above all in the sacraments. Jesus Christ, "the same yesterday and today and for ever" is God's "now".

21. The liturgical year thus suggests the sovereignty of the grace of Christ. We say that we "follow" or "observe" the liturgical year, but this Year of Grace also carries us along. Once we enter it faithfully we must allow it to determine the shape of our daily lives. It sets up a series of "appointments" with the Lord. We know there are set days, moments and occasions when he expects us. Within this framework of obligation, duty and covenant, we are part of something greater than ourselves. We can detect a sense of being sustained or borne forward by the power and pace of a sacred cycle that is beyond our control. It will run its course whether we like it or not. This should give us an awareness of the divine dimension of the liturgical year as an expression of the power and authority of Jesus, who is the Lord of history. As the blessing of the Paschal candle recalls: "All time belongs to him and all the ages." The sacred cycle thus becomes a sacrament of God's time. Salvation history is among us here and now. This time is his offer of grace.

22. Considered from one aspect this awareness of time can be intimidating. But it should be interpreted in the perspective of a spirituality of divine Providence. Awareness that "my time" rests in God's hands is a call to trust, to faith, to letting go of self. The Jesuit director Jean-Pierre de Caussade proposed this as a "self-abandonment to divine providence". Once time is recognized as salvation history, once each passing day or week is seen as sacred time, it is easier

for us to review our relationship with the Lord of time and to let time pass into his hands.

23. Sacred time also gives us a strong sense of being members of the Church. I have already observed how our sense of time is reshaped by the subtle catechesis of each liturgical year. We become conscious of this especially when we are called to teach the faith to children and young people. Any perusal of catechetical texts shows the pedagogical value of liturgical time. The same catechetical opportunities are available to the clergy in preaching and teaching during the liturgy, above all in drawing out the meaning of the major rites and ceremonies described in this book.

24. The liturgical year is a means of evangelization. Stories of conversion often include references to Christian feast days that were key moments in the personal process. A critical event may have begun with an invitation to enter a totally unfamiliar experience. Someone is taken to Christmas midnight Mass in a Catholic church, and that experience ultimately leads to Catholic faith. But returning to the faith is also made easier through sacred time. Even the most casual members of the Church recall their Catholic identity when the time comes around each year for the observance of Christmas and Easter. On those days, many fallen-away Catholics know that the Lord awaits them, and they know where he waits, even if they do not feel inclined to respond to his invitation. But the liturgical year and its vivid rites gently open other doors for them to return to the life of grace. Anyone can accept the blessed ashes on Ash Wednesday. The greatest sinner can come forward to venerate the cross on Good Friday. These simple acts of penance pave the way to a good confession, that is, the recovery of the grace of Baptism that leads to the altar of the Eucharist.

25. The evangelical dimension of the Year of Grace is one rationale behind the two major seasons of preparation and conversion, Advent and Lent. As already noted, Advent originated in the third century in Gaul, where it was an alternative time for preparing catechumens for Baptism, given on January 6, the Epiphany. In Rome this form of Advent became a season of preparation for the feasts of Christmas and the Epiphany. Today we maintain the emphasis of the Roman tradition, but the anticipation of the Incarnation calls for interior preparation and conversion.

26. Testimony to the penitential observance of Lent is found in Saint Athanasius and other Fathers, and the forty days was well established by the fourth century, although Sundays were counted as part of this cycle. Ash Wednesday and the three days that follow it were added later so that the forty days could be weekdays because Sunday is never a day for fasting. The seasons of penance and preparation remind us that God's past events are present in our events, refashioning our lives in the continuous process of conversion to Christ.

The Divine Future

27. The future orientation of the liturgical year is best appreciated in the light of pastoral opportunities. The attentive celebrant of the liturgy and sacraments assists the faithful to celebrate Christian time by remembering past events that embody a saving offer of grace here and now. But the future offers another possibility for his pastoral use of time. He should encourage his people to look forward, through and beyond the transitory moments of this life, to the *telos*, to the finality and purpose of it all. As a pastor, he is leading his people towards the *eschaton*, to the goal and beatific fulfillment of our journey through time to eternity. That is the eschatological meaning of the annual cycles of

Christian seasons and celebrations. It is also the reason Christians have traditionally turned to pray towards the East, where the dawn of Christ lights this world in anticipation of his eternal Day. Like liturgical orientation, the Church year points beyond itself. It is never an end in itself. It constantly speaks of eternity. Each year recapitulates the Christian's journey towards heaven. Each year is another dawn containing the eternal Day.

28. The liturgical year is eschatological in a basic sense because it reveals how reality moves forward in a specific way. The history of the universe is not merely a series of great cycles, of going back to the beginning and starting all over again. Indeed a relentless understanding of time as repetitive cycles is pagan rather than Christian. Our Judaeo-Christian understanding of time is *teleological*, that is, as progressing towards a goal, an end, to God.

29. In considering the teleological way we view the flow of time, we should read the "signs of the times" in the twenty-first century and sharpen our perception of the current erosion of faith and reason. As the era of old ideologies recedes, people in our complex societies are taking up a variety of contrasting world views, for example "post-modern" forms of irrationalism are being challenged by a revived rationalist scientism. Either of these trends may be accompanied by an underlying secularist ideology of dogmatic individualism, which justifies gross selfishness. But it is interesting to reflect how these world views all include a misunderstanding of the meaning and purpose of time.

30. It is obvious to Christians that post-modernism in various forms of secularism is nihilism. Nothing is valued. Nothing has inherent meaning. The human person has no value, no inherent dignity or rights. We are lost in an indiffer-

ent process of time where we do not matter, where life is seen as one experience following another in a meaningless succession of variable sensations. By contrast, the irrational neo-paganism of the "new age" includes the revival of a cyclic understanding of reality but also another basic misunderstanding of reality. In a cyclic understanding of time and reality the error of reincarnation flourishes, and with it the dignity, value and uniqueness of the human person are eroded. The rise of the "new age" phenomenon may not be merely a passing phase, as we might have imagined some years ago. It bears within it a fatalism and a determinism that undermine moral responsibility and thus create indifference. The "new age" is as ethically bankrupt as secularist individualism. Its forms and disciplines are soft and permissive. It tolerates evil and can even conjure it up.

31. Christianity offers an alternative vision of the future in terms not only of a progress towards a goal but of a choice. There will be a point of resolution for my past, a moment of judgment. This is brought to us in the *apocalyptic* quality of the liturgical year, which bears the message "The Lord is coming again." Faced with the prospect that "he will come again to judge the living and the dead", we are reminded of a series of challenging truths revealed in Jesus Christ: We are responsible beings; our actions in time have eternal repercussions; each of us is taken seriously by a personal God who loves us; our life span and all time bear his purpose. Therefore we will be called to give an account of our temporal lives when we return to our Creator.

32. Eternal life thus raises the question of the end of our allotted time or the meaning of death. In this regard, November is an important month in the liturgical year, offering opportunities for catechesis and preaching. While All Souls Day is described as the "commemoration of all the faithful

departed", it is not so much an occasion for looking back over the lives of dead people as a challenge to look forward to where they—and we—are going. Praying for the souls in purgatory brings with it a sense of the future, our future, even if this is only the passing thought, "But will someone remember me when I die and need prayers?" Purgatory also seems to be a kind of halfway house between this life and the next, that is, between time and eternity. Speculative theology raises the question of a kind of "time" in purgatory because it is a merciful process, or a progress into what C. S. Lewis called "deep heaven". Purgatory is surely the most intensely teleological "moment" in the future that awaits us beyond the death we all must experience.

33.   Prayer for the dead is a dimension of our faith in the Communion of Saints that we profess in the Apostles' Creed. This Communion is an understanding of the Church that helps us look beyond time to another great truth we proclaim in the Nicene Creed, "the resurrection of the body and life everlasting". The Communion of Saints runs through the liturgical year in the "sanctoral cycle" of familiar solemnities, feasts, memorials and commemorations in honor of saints, above all those associated with Our Blessed Lady, the Queen of Saints. There is a catechetical or homiletic value in marking these saints' days and setting up their lives as good examples of virtue and cooperation with grace. But as we seek their intercession we also reinforce the sense of being surrounded by a "great cloud of witnesses". They point to the future as they encourage us in our journey towards eternity. They remind us what that journey will entail in terms of participating in the renewal of the whole cosmos, the general resurrection of the dead and restoration of all things in Christ. The saints are already "there", in eternity, welcoming us into the divine future.

34. As the millennium celebrations unfolded and ushered in January 1, A.D. 2000, a strange incident occurred in Australia. It was seen on television by millions all around the world, but it was not widely comprehended. The famous Sydney Harbour Bridge was being used as the framework for a spectacular display of fireworks. Suddenly, the colors faded, and in blazing white letters the fireworks formed one word: *Eternity*. Everyone in that city knew what it meant, not theologically of course, but at least as a fragment of their local history. Many years ago a somewhat eccentric man was converted to Christianity. He spent the rest of his life on a simple mission—scrawling that word *Eternity* on the walls of his city. He wanted to remind people, to make them face God's present moment, to point them beyond time to the real future. Ultimately that is what the liturgical year does. It transforms our time into a sacrament of eternity.

Christ yesterday and today,
the beginning and the end,
Alpha and Omega,
all time belongs to him
and all the ages.

— Blessing and Preparation of the Paschal Candle

The General
Roman Calendar

35. (Proper Calendars for the Dioceses of the United States of America, Great Britain and other countries are found in appendix 8.)

JANUARY

1.	Octave of Christmas	
	SOLEMNITY OF MARY, MOTHER OF GOD	Solemnity
2.	Basil the Great and Gregory Nazianzen,	
	bishops and doctors	Memorial
3.	*Holy Name of Jesus* *	
4.		
5.		
6.		
7.	*Raymond of Penyafort, priest*	
8.		
9.		
10.		
11.		
12.		
13.	*Hilary, bishop and doctor*	
14.		
15.		
16.		
17.	Anthony, abbot	Memorial
18.		

* When no rank is given, it is an optional memorial.

19.		
20.	*Fabian, pope and martyr* *Sebastian, martyr*	
21.	Agnes, virgin and martyr	Memorial
22.	*Vincent, deacon and martyr*	
23.		
24.	Francis de Sales, bishop and doctor	Memorial
25.	Conversion of Paul, apostle	Feast
26.	Timothy and Titus, bishops	Memorial
27.	*Angela Merici, virgin*	
28.	Thomas Aquinas, priest and doctor	Memorial
29.		
30.		
31.	John Bosco, priest	Memorial
Sunday between January 2 and January 8: EPIPHANY		Solemnity
Sunday after Epiphany: Baptism of the Lord		Feast

FEBRUARY

1.		
2.	Presentation of the Lord	Feast
3.	*Blaise, bishop and martyr* *Ansgar, bishop*	
4.		
5.	Agatha, virgin and martyr	Memorial
6.	Paul Miki and companions, martyrs	Memorial
7.		
8.	*Jerome Emiliani* *Josephine Bakhita, virgin*	
9.		
10.	Scholastica, virgin	Memorial

11. *Our Lady of Lourdes*

12.

13.

14. Cyril, monk, and Methodius, bishop   Memorial

15.

16.

17. *Seven Founders of the Order of Servites*

18.

19.

20.

21. *Peter Damian, bishop and doctor*

22. Chair of Peter, apostle   Feast

23. Polycarp, bishop and martyr   Memorial

24.

25.

26.

27.

28.

MARCH

1.

2.

3.

4. *Casimir*

5.

6.

7. Perpetua and Felicity, martyrs   Memorial

8. *John of God, religious*

9. *Frances of Rome, religious*

10.

11.

12.

18

13.
14.
15.
16.
17. *Patrick, bishop*
18. *Cyril of Jerusalem, bishop and doctor*
19. JOSEPH, HUSBAND OF MARY   Solemnity
20.
21.
22.
23. *Turibius de Mogrovejo, bishop*
24.
25. ANNUNCIATION   Solemnity
26.
27.
28.
29.
30.
31.

APRIL

1.
2. *Francis of Paola, hermit*
3.
4. *Isidore, bishop and doctor*
5. *Vincent Ferrer, priest*
6.
7. John Baptist de la Salle, priest   Memorial
8.
9.
10.
11. Stanislaus, bishop and martyr   Memorial

12.

13. *Martin I, pope and martyr*

14.

15.

16.

17.

18.

19.

20.

21. *Anselm, bishop and doctor*

22.

23. *George, martyr*
    Adalbert, bishop and martyr

24. *Fidelis of Sigmaringen, priest and martyr*

25. Mark, evangelist   Feast

26.

27.

28. *Peter Chanel, priest and martyr*
    Louis Marie Grignion de Montfort, priest

29. Catherine of Siena, virgin and doctor   Memorial

30. *Pius V, pope*

MAY

1. *Joseph the Worker*

2. Athanasius, bishop and doctor   Memorial

3. Philip and James, apostles   Feast

4.

5.

6.

7.

8.

9.

10.

11.

12. *Nereus and Achilleus, martyrs*
    Pancras, martyr

13. *Our Lady of Fatima*

14. Matthias, apostle   Feast

15.

16.

17.

18. *John I, pope and martyr*

19.

20. *Bernardine of Siena, priest*

21. *Christopher Magallanes, priest, and his companions,*
    martyrs

22. *Rita of Cascia, religious*

23.

24.

25. *Venerable Bede, priest and doctor*
    Gregory VII, pope
    Mary Magdalene de Pazzi, virgin

26. Philip Neri, priest   Memorial

27. *Augustine of Canterbury, bishop*

28.

29.

30.

31. Visitation   Feast

First Sunday after Pentecost: HOLY TRINITY   Solemnity

Thursday after Holy Trinity: THE BODY AND
   BLOOD OF CHRIST   Solemnity

JUNE

1.	Justin, martyr	Memorial
2.	*Marcellinus and Peter, martyrs*	
3.	Charles Lwanga and companions, martyrs	Memorial
4.		
5.	Boniface, bishop and martyr	Memorial
6.	*Norbert, bishop*	
7.		
8.		
9.	*Ephrem, deacon and doctor*	
10.		
11.	Barnabas, apostle	Memorial
12.		
13.	Anthony of Padua, priest and doctor	Memorial
14.		
15.		
16.		
17.		
18.		
19.	*Romuald, abbot*	
20.		
21.	Aloysius Gonzaga, religious	Memorial
22.	*Paulinus of Nola, bishop* *John Fisher, bishop and martyr, and* *Thomas More, martyr*	
23.		
24.	BIRTH OF JOHN THE BAPTIST	Solemnity
25.		
26.		
27.	*Cyril of Alexandria, bishop and doctor*	
28.	Irenaeus, bishop and martyr	Memorial

29. PETER AND PAUL, APOSTLES   Solemnity
30. *First Martyrs of the Church of Rome*
Friday following Second Sunday after Pentecost:
   SACRED HEART   Solemnity
Saturday after the Second Sunday after Pentecost:
   Immaculate Heart of Mary   Memorial

JULY

1.
2.
3. Thomas, apostle   Feast
4. *Elizabeth of Portugal*
5. *Anthony Zaccaria, priest*
6. *Maria Goretti, virgin and martyr*
7.
8.
9. *Augustine Zhao Rong, priest, and companions,
      martyrs*
10.
11. Benedict, abbot   Memorial
12.
13. *Henry*
14. *Camillus de Lellis, priest*
15. Bonaventure, bishop and doctor   Memorial
16. *Our Lady of Mount Carmel*
17.
18.
19.
20. *Apollinaris, bishop and martyr*
21. *Lawrence of Brindisi, priest and doctor*
22. Mary Magdalene   Memorial

23. *Bridget, religious*
24. *Charbel Makhluf, priest*
25. James, apostle   Feast
26. Joachim and Ann, parents of Mary   Memorial
27.
28.
29. Martha   Memorial
30. *Peter Chrysologus, bishop and doctor*
31. Ignatius of Loyola, priest   Memorial

AUGUST

1. Alphonsus Liguori, bishop and doctor   Memorial
2. *Eusebius of Vercelli, bishop*
   Peter Julian Eymard, priest
3.
4. John Vianney, priest   Memorial
5. *Dedication of Saint Mary Major*
6. Transfiguration   Feast
7. *Sixtus II, pope and martyr, and*
   companions, martyrs
   Cajetan, priest
8. Dominic, priest   Memorial
9. *Teresa Benedicta of the Cross, virgin and martyr*
10. Lawrence, deacon and martyr   Feast
11. Clare, virgin   Memorial
12. *Jane Frances de Chantal, religious*
13. *Pontian, pope and martyr, and Hippolytus,*
    priest and martyr
14. Maximilian Mary Kolbe, priest and martyr   Memorial
15. ASSUMPTION   Solemnity
16. *Stephen of Hungary*

17.

18.

19. *John Eudes, priest*

20. Bernard, abbot and doctor — Memorial

21. Pius X, pope — Memorial

22. Queenship of Mary — Memorial

23. *Rose of Lima, virgin*

24. Bartholomew, apostle — Feast

25. *Louis*
   Joseph Calasanz, priest

26.

27. Monica — Memorial

28. Augustine, bishop and doctor — Memorial

29. Beheading of John the Baptist, martyr — Memorial

30.

31.

SEPTEMBER

1.

2.

3. Gregory the Great, pope and doctor — Memorial

4.

5.

6.

7.

8. Birth of Mary — Feast

9. *Peter Claver, priest*

10.

11.

12. *The Holy Name of Mary*

13. John Chrysostom, bishop and doctor — Memorial

14. Triumph of the Cross — Feast

15.	Our Lady of Sorrows	Memorial
16.	Cornelius, pope and martyr, and Cyprian, bishop and martyr	Memorial
17.	*Robert Bellarmine, bishop and doctor*	
18.		
19.	*Januarius, bishop and martyr*	
20.	Andrew Kim Tae-gon, priest, Paul Chong Ha-sang, and companions, martyrs	Memorial
21.	Matthew, apostle and evangelist	Feast
22.		
23.		
24.		
25.		
26.	*Cosmas and Damian, martyrs*	
27.	Vincent de Paul, priest	Memorial
28.	*Wenceslaus, martyr* *Lawrence Ruiz and companions, martyrs*	
29.	Michael, Gabriel, and Raphael, archangels	Feast
30.	Jerome, priest and doctor	Memorial

OCTOBER

1.	Theresa of the Child Jesus, virgin	Memorial
2.	Guardian Angels	Memorial
3.		
4.	Francis of Assisi	Memorial
5.		
6.	*Bruno, priest*	
7.	Our Lady of the Rosary	Memorial
8.		
9.	*Denis, bishop and martyr, and companions, martyrs* *John Leonardi, priest*	

10.

11.

12.

13.

14. *Callistus I, pope and martyr*

15. Teresa of Jesus, virgin and doctor   Memorial

16. *Hedwig, religious*
    Margaret Mary Alacoque, virgin

17. Ignatius of Antioch, bishop and martyr   Memorial

18. Luke, evangelist   Feast

19. Isaac Jogues and John de Brébeuf, priests and
        martyrs, and companions, martyrs   Memorial
    Paul of the Cross, priest

20.

21.

22.

23. *John of Capistrano, priest*

24. *Anthony Mary Claret, bishop*

25.

26.

27.

28. Simon and Jude, apostles   Feast

29.

30.

31.

NOVEMBER

1. ALL SAINTS   Solemnity

2. ALL SOULS

3. *Martin de Porres, religious*

4. Charles Borromeo, bishop   Memorial

5.

6.

7.

8.

9.   Dedication of Saint John Lateran   Feast

10.   Leo the Great, pope and doctor   Memorial

11.   Martin of Tours, bishop   Memorial

12.   Josaphat, bishop and martyr   Memorial

13.

14.

15.   *Albert the Great, bishop and doctor*

16.   *Margaret of Scotland*
      Gertrude, virgin

17.   Elizabeth of Hungary, religious   Memorial

18.   *Dedication of the churches of Peter and Paul, apostles*

19.

20.

21.   Presentation of Mary   Memorial

22.   Cecilia, virgin and martyr   Memorial

23.   *Clement I, pope and martyr*
      Columban, abbot

24.   *Andrew Dung-Lac, priest, and companions, martyrs*

25.   *Catherine of Alexandria, virgin and martyr*

26.

27.

28.

29.

30.   Andrew, apostle   Feast

Last Sunday in Ordinary Time:
      CHRIST THE KING   Solemnity

DECEMBER

1.		
2.		
3.	Francis Xavier, priest	Memorial
4.	*John Damascene, priest and doctor*	
5.		
6.	*Nicholas, bishop*	
7.	Ambrose, bishop and doctor	Memorial
8.	IMMACULATE CONCEPTION	Solemnity
9.		
10.		
11.	*Damasus I, pope*	
12.		
13.	Lucy, virgin and martyr	Memorial
14.	John of the Cross, priest and doctor	Memorial
15.		
16.		
17.		
18.		
19.		
20.		
21.	*Peter Canisius, priest and doctor*	
22.		
23.	*John of Kanty, priest*	
24.		
25.	CHRISTMAS	Solemnity
26.	Stephen, first martyr	Feast
27.	John, apostle and evangelist	Feast
28.	Holy Innocents, martyrs	Feast

29. *Thomas Becket, bishop and martyr*

30.

31. *Sylvester I, pope*

Sunday within the octave of Christmas or if there is
no Sunday within the octave, December 30: Holy Family   Feast

I.

General Norms for the Liturgical Year

36. The liturgical year begins on the First Sunday of Advent. Sunday is the first day of the liturgical week. A liturgical day runs from midnight to midnight. However, the celebration of Sundays and solemnities begins with First Vespers on the evening of the day before.[1]

37. *Sunday* is the primordial Christian feast, the weekly paschal celebration, observed by the Universal Church according to apostolic tradition.[2] Sunday is the "Easter which returns week by week, celebrating Christ's victory over sin and death, the fulfillment in him of the first creation and the dawn of the 'new creation' ".[3] The celebration of Sunday gives way only to solemnities or feasts of the Lord. However, the Sundays of Advent, Lent and the Easter Season always take precedence over all solemnities or feasts of the Lord. Therefore, solemnities that fall on these Sundays are observed on another day, as indicated in the annual Ordo published by an episcopal conference, diocese or religious order. The Nicene Creed is sung or said at Mass on all Sundays, and the Gloria is sung on most Sundays, but it is omitted on Sundays in Advent and Lent. The Te Deum is

---

[1] Cf. *General Norms for the Liturgical Year and the Calendar* (henceforth LY), no. 3.

[2] Cf. LY, no. 4; *Code of Canon Law* (henceforth CIC), Canon 1244 §1.

[3] John Paul II, Apostolic Letter *Dies Domini* (May 31, 1998), 1.

included in the Office of Readings on Sundays, except on the Sundays in Lent.

38. *Solemnities* are regarded as the most important days in the calendar and begin with First Vespers on the evening of the day before. In the Roman Missal, some solemnities also have their own vigil Mass to be celebrated on the evening of the day before.[4] The Gloria and Creed are sung or said at Mass on all solemnities. The Te Deum is included in the Office of Readings. The night office is one of the two forms of Sunday Compline, with the appropriate closing prayer.

39. *Feasts* do not have a First Vespers because they are celebrated within the limits of the liturgical day. However, whenever a feast of the Lord in the universal calendar (e.g., the Transfiguration) falls on a Sunday in the Season of the Year or the Christmas Season, then the propers of that feast replace the Sunday Mass and Divine Office.[5] At Mass on a feast, the Gloria is sung or said.[6] (The Creed is sung or said only if there is a good pastoral reason for including it.) The Te Deum is included in the Office of Readings. The night office is Compline of the appropriate weekday, although a Sunday Compline may be used, with the closing Compline prayer for solemnities that do not fall on Sundays.

40. *Memorials* are either obligatory or optional. As explained below, in chapter 11, "The Season of the Year", their celebration is regulated by the norms of the Missal and the Liturgy of the Hours. Obligatory memorials that fall on the weekdays of Lent are commemorated as optional memorials. When several optional memorials occur on the same

---

[4] Cf. LY, no. 11.
[5] Cf. LY, no. 13.
[6] Cf. *General Instruction of the Roman Missal* (revised edition, 2000, henceforth GIRM), no. 53.

day, only one is to be celebrated in the Mass and Liturgy of the Hours. The Gloria and Creed are not sung or said on memorials, and the Te Deum is not included in the Office of Readings. The night office is Compline of the appropriate weekday, or a Sunday form of Compline, as for feasts above.

41. Only the Pope can regulate sacred time in terms of establishing, transferring or suppressing holy days or days of penance that apply to the Universal Church. However, the diocesan bishop can proclaim special feast days or days of penance within his diocese or territory, but only for specific occasions.[7] Apart from Sundays, the universal holy days of obligation are: Christmas Day, the Epiphany, the Ascension, Corpus Christi, the Solemnity of the Mother of God (January 1), the Immaculate Conception, the Assumption, and the solemnities of Saint Joseph (March 19), Saints Peter and Paul (June 29) and All Saints (November 1). However, with the prior approval of the Holy See, episcopal conferences may suppress certain holy days of obligation or transfer them to a Sunday.[8] The universal days of penance are each Friday of the year and the season of Lent.[9]

> The whole mystery of Christ, from his Incarnation to the day of Pentecost and the expectation of his coming again, is recalled by the Church during the course of the year.
>
> — *General Norms for the Liturgical Year and the Calendar*, no. 17.

---

[7] Cf. CIC, Canon 1244 §2.
[8] Cf. CIC, Canon 1246.
[9] Cf. CIC, Canon 1250.

2.

Advent and Christmas

42. The season with which the liturgical year begins is not penitential. Advent is a time of preparation and reflection, hope and anticipation. The coming of the eternal Son of God is celebrated in the three ways we experience time: past, present and future. He came for us in our flesh through the Incarnation; he comes to us in the Church through grace; he will come at the end of time to judge us, living or dead.

43. Advent focuses on the key persons who were prepared and chosen by God to make possible the Incarnation of his Son Jesus Christ. Our eyes are drawn to Mary Immaculate, Saint John the Baptist, Saint Joseph and Saints Elizabeth and Zechariah. The prophecies of Isaiah run through the continuous readings, pointing always to the coming of the Anointed One. From the first Sunday of the season, the Liturgy of the Hours builds up a sense of expectation, promise and hope. Advent is also the season for reflecting on the "last things" of the future: death, judgment, heaven and hell. Preaching and catechesis on eschatology is essential at this time.[1]

---

[1] See *Catechism of the Catholic Church* (henceforth CCC): on death, nos. 1005–14, 1021; on heaven, nos. 1023–29; on hell, nos. 1033–37; on purgatory, nos. 1030–32; on the last judgment, nos. 1038–41 and 668–78; the new heaven and new earth, nos. 1042–50.

Sundays in Advent

44. Although the Sundays in Advent rank as solemnities, the Gloria is not sung or said at Mass. The third edition of the Roman Missal provides propers for the weekday Masses in Advent. Unlike Lent, there is no restriction on the use of the organ and other musical instruments during this season. The altar may be decorated with flowers, although their use should be moderate so as to highlight the solemnity of Christmas.[2] The violet vestments and antependia used during Advent may be different in design from those used for Lent.[3] Rose vestments may be used on the Third Sunday in Advent (Gaudete Sunday),[4] and on that day the antependia on the altar and ambo and the tabernacle veil may also be of this color.

45. In some churches it is the custom to set up an "Advent wreath" in or near the sanctuary. This may take the form of four large candles arranged amidst the greenery of a wreath or on candlesticks. A candle is lit to mark each of the four Sundays of the season so that the four are burning on the Fourth Sunday.[5] But this wreath does not replace the liturgical altar candles, and, because it is an optional custom,

---

[2] Cf. GIRM, no. 305. The revised GIRM adds that when they adorn the altar, flowers should be placed *around* rather than directly *on* the altar.

[3] The difference is best registered through symbols, e.g., avoiding instruments of the Passion, or through contrasting colored orphreys, etc., but the basic color remains the same, "violet", that is, a bright purple (cf. *Ceremonies of the Modern Roman Rite* [henceforth CMRR], no. 132). Blue is not the color for Advent, notwithstanding the late medieval use of this color in some dioceses.

[4] Cf. GIRM, no. 346f. and CMRR, no. 134.

[5] Representing the four Sundays with three violet candles and one pink candle (for Gaudete Sunday) is customary.

there is no official rite for lighting the candles. It is customary in some places for the wreath to be blessed on the First Sunday of Advent.

The Immaculate Conception, December 8

46. This solemnity is one of the greatest feasts of Our Lady and thus remains a holy day of obligation in many countries. Preaching and catechesis should concentrate on the purpose and meaning of the Immaculate Conception.[6] A solemn novena in preparation for December 8 may be customary.[7] The Advent theme should be worked into this novena, which also provides an opportunity for the faithful to benefit from the ministry of visiting preachers and confessors.

Preparing for Christmas

47. From December 17, the Advent Season enters its final phase, evident in the rich liturgical texts provided in the Missal and breviary for the eight days before Christmas, especially the "O antiphons". The weekday Advent Masses take precedence over any memorials of the saints, which can only be celebrated in a limited way as commemorations.[8] A solemn novena may lead to Christmas, incorporated in the daily celebrations of the Mass, the Liturgy of the Hours and eucharistic adoration. Pastors should provide a wide range of opportunities so that the faithful have ready access to the Sacrament of Penance in the weeks and days preceding

---

[6] See CCC, nos. 411, 484–93, 721–26, and on original sin, nos. 396–412.

[7] In some churches an image of Mary Immaculate is set up in or near the sanctuary during the novena.

[8] As set out in GIRM, no. 355 a, and the *Norms for the Liturgy of the Hours*, nos. 237–39.

Christmas.[9] Therefore, celebrations of the Second Rite of Reconciliation may well be organized through deaneries or other pastoral regions to ensure an adequate supply of confessors.

48. Carols are a popular part of the Christmas Season and are usually anticipated some time before December 25. Strictly speaking, this rich musical treasury of incarnational theology and devotion should not be introduced into the liturgy before the vigil of Christmas, commercial customs notwithstanding. Nevertheless, during late Advent, a para-liturgical "festival of carols" may be a fruitful ecumenical occasion, celebrated in a church or in a public place if the weather permits. In a Catholic church, such a festival of carols should appropriately conclude with eucharistic adoration and Benediction.[10]

Christmas

49. While the Solemnity of the Birth of Our Savior in fact ranks after Easter and Pentecost, it remains the most popular celebration of the Church year, focused on our wonder at the sublime mystery of the Incarnation. The Masses of Christ's Nativity should be celebrated as solemnly as possible, with the best white or gold vestments, the finest vessels, with incense and the extra flowers, candles and lamps that are customary on this festival.

---

[9] Careful provision should be made for bringing the Eucharist to those confined at home or in hospitals, etc., during Christmas, but their desire to go to confession at this time should not be forgotten.

[10] "Adeste Fideles" would be an appropriate choice for the hymn of adoration before Benediction.

50. There are four Masses for Christmas, each with its own distinctive propers and readings: the Vigil Mass, Mass at Midnight, Mass at Dawn and Mass during the Day. All priests may celebrate or concelebrate three Masses, "provided that they are celebrated at their proper times".[11] When the bishop or the episcopal conference indicates that the Vigil Mass may fulfil the obligation, it could well be celebrated as a family Mass, especially for those unable to come to Mass at Midnight.

51. The sung Office of Readings may appropriately precede the Mass at Midnight and may even be joined to it.[12] Mass at Dawn is in effect the first morning Mass of Christmas Day. The Mass during the Day is used for all other Eucharistic Celebrations. During the Creed at the Christmas Masses all kneel at the words "by the power of the Holy Spirit . . . man."[13] It would seem appropriate for the celebrant and deacon(s) to kneel before the altar, or at least to kneel in the direction of the altar. When the First Eucharistic Prayer is chosen, the variation at "In union with the whole Church . . ." is used during the four Masses of Christmas and throughout the Octave of Christmas.

---

[11] Cf. *Roman Missal*, third typical edition, 2002 (henceforth MR), Christmas, Vigil Mass. This means that it is no longer permissible to celebrate the three Masses one after the other, at any hour. However, according to Canon 951 §1, a stipend may be accepted for all three Masses.

[12] See CMRR, no. 773. Alternatively, the choir may lead a non-liturgical service of carols before Mass, during which priests should be available for confessions. Ideally midnight Mass should begin at midnight, but often the timing has to be adjusted to meet local conditions. Nevertheless, the title "Mass at Midnight" and its proper texts should be reserved only for a Mass celebrated late in the night.

[13] Preferably during the homily, the people should be reminded and instructed about this act of reverence for the Eternal Word who humbled himself to take our flesh and come among us.

The Proclamation of the Birth of Christ

52. In the Roman Martyrology a formal announcement or proclamation of the birth of Christ is provided for Christmas Day. The proclamation sets the birth of Our Savior in the context of salvation history, relating the Incarnation to the people and events of history. For the text, see appendix 4, "The Proclamation of the Birth of Christ". This should be sung from the ambo, by a deacon, cantor or a reader. Unless the deacon is already wearing a dalmatic, he wears a white cope. A cantor or reader wears an alb or cassock and surplice. Lacking this personnel, the celebrant, a concelebrant (in eucharistic vestments) or another priest (in a white cope) may sing or proclaim it. All stand during this proclamation.

53. There are several options for the timing of this proclamation. The preferable moment would be during the extended Office of Readings before midnight Mass, just before the Te Deum. It could also be included as part of a para-liturgy or service of carols before midnight Mass, preferably as the culmination of such a celebration. Alternatively, it may be sung after the opening of the office at Morning Prayer or Vespers, that is, before the office hymn. In the U.S., the proclamation may follow the greeting and introduction to the Mass, and it then takes the place of the Penitential Rite. It may be used at any or all of the Christmas Masses. The deacon or cantor does not seek a blessing from the celebrant before the proclamation, but the celebrant should briefly introduce it, explaining how it celebrates God's promises that are fulfilled in salvation history.

The Crib

54. The Christmas crib has become a universal custom in the Roman Rite. It is set up on December 17 or just before First Vespers of Christmas, but the image of the Christ Child should not be placed there until before midnight Mass or before the Office of Readings, if this is joined to the Mass. However, the placing of the Christ Child may be carried out before the vigil Mass where this is a family celebration, and then the rite could be repeated before midnight Mass. The image may be placed in the crib without any ceremony. However, according to the custom observed at Bethlehem, the image may be placed in the crib during an act of public devotion preceding the liturgy. This act could take the following forms.

55. With appropriate singing or music, the liturgical procession comes from the sacristy. Wearing eucharistic vestments or a cope (conveniently held back by deacon[s] or servers), the celebrant carries the image, which may rest on a noble cushion. On arrival at the crib, he kneels and puts it in the appropriate place.[14] Incense is prepared, and the crib may be incensed, and/or a short rite of the blessing of the crib may be celebrated. Then the entrance antiphon or hymn begins, and the procession proceeds to the altar. If the cope is worn, it is best removed and replaced by the chasuble, after the incensation of the altar, when the celebrant goes to the chair.

56. According to a simpler alternative, the servers, deacon(s) and celebrant enter as usual during the entrance antiphon

---

[14] In some places the celebrant enters without the image of the Christ Child and waits in front of the altar or crib while a family or some children bring the image to him to be placed in the crib.

or hymn. Then the procession pauses briefly at the crib to allow the celebrant to place the image there before continuing to the altar.[15] The crib should not be set up directly under or in front of the altar, unless the church is very small and there is no other suitable place. In some parishes, it is customary to encourage the children to bring gifts to the crib to be distributed to poor children.

Octave of Christmas

57. In the modern Roman Calendar only Christmas and Easter enjoy the privilege of an octave, that is, extending the celebration of the solemnity throughout the following seven days. The Christmas Octave is somewhat different from that of Easter insofar as it includes some significant feasts: Saint Stephen the Proto-martyr (December 26), Saint John the Evangelist (December 27), the Holy Innocents (December 28, a day of prayer for the rights of the unborn in some places). The Solemnity of the Holy Family is celebrated on the Sunday in the Octave of Christmas, or December 30 when Christmas falls on a Sunday, and this obviously provides a good occasion to preach and catechize on the nature, mission and rights of the Christian family.[16]

58. Whether or not it is observed as a holy day of obligation, the Solemnity of Mary, Mother of God, January 1, offers an occasion for preaching and catechesis on the meaning of Mary's greatest title.[17] It also marks the beginning of the calendar year, which raises some interesting pastoral problems. Religious celebrations of the New Year should be planned prudently, taking into account local conditions and other

---

[15] This would be more appropriate in a small church where the crib is set up in the sanctuary.

[16] See CCC, nos. 1655–58, 1882, 2201–33.

[17] See CCC, nos. 494–507, 721–26.

ways of marking the occasion. Celebrating a Mass at midnight may not always be appropriate, and this may seem best reserved for Christmas, but the New Year might appropriately commence with a vigil of prayer and solemn eucharistic adoration. In many places, this would only be feasible in a peaceful ambience, such as a religious community or a place of pilgrimage.

Epiphany

59. The Solemnity of the Epiphany is celebrated either on January 6 or, according to the decision of the episcopal conference, on the Sunday between January 2 and January 8. The young Messiah is revealed as the light of the nations. Yet, as the antiphon for the Magnificat at Second Vespers reminds us, three mysteries are encompassed in this solemnity: the adoration of the Christ Child by the Magi, the Baptism of Christ and the wedding feast at Cana. When the First Eucharistic Prayer is chosen, the variation at "In union with the whole Church . . ." is used. Extra candles and/or lamps may be placed around the sanctuary and in other parts of the church to honor Christ revealed as the Light of the Gentiles.[18] It is customary to replace the images of the shepherds at the crib with the three Magi and their gifts. On the vigil of the Epiphany, in some communities it is also customary to bless "Epiphany water" for the blessing of homes at this time.[19]

---

[18] Cf. *Ceremonial of Bishops* (henceforth CB), no. 240.

[19] The solemn rite is found in the preconciliar *Rituale Romanum*: IX, ix, 28. According to a central European custom, chalk is also blessed so that the year and the initials of the Magi may be inscribed above the door of each dwelling that has been blessed.

The Proclamation of the Date of Easter on Epiphany

60. To remind us that the whole liturgical year takes its meaning from the risen Savior, the ancient custom of proclaiming the date of Easter and the movable feasts should be maintained during the celebration of the Epiphany of the Lord. (The proper dates for Ash Wednesday, Easter, Ascension, Pentecost and the First Sunday of Advent are taken from the current Ordo or from the table of movable feasts included with introductory documents in the Roman Missal.) These dates are inserted into the text that is provided in appendix 5, "The Proclamation of the Date of Easter on Epiphany". The dates are simply the *day* and *month*, e.g., "the third of April". This proclamation should be sung from the ambo, by a deacon, cantor or a reader. Unless the deacon is already wearing a dalmatic, he wears a white cope. A cantor or reader wears an alb or cassock and surplice. Lacking this personnel, the celebrant or a concelebrant (in eucharistic vestments) or another priest (in a white cope) may sing or proclaim it. All stand during this proclamation.

61. The proclamation takes place after the Gospel, the homily or the Prayer after Communion. It is customary to sing it only at the principal Mass of the Epiphany, but for pastoral reasons it may well be used at other Masses. The deacon or cantor does not seek a blessing from the celebrant before the proclamation of the feasts, but the celebrant should briefly introduce it, explaining why this gracious custom is still maintained in an age when we all have calendars, that is, to remind us how the whole Christian year leads up to and focuses on the Resurrection of the Lord.

62. The Season of the Year commences on the day after the Baptism of the Lord. Green vestments are worn on Sundays and ferial days. The Season of the Year continues until

the Tuesday before Ash Wednesday, inclusive. It will commence once again on the Monday after Pentecost.

Prayer for Christian Unity

63. In many countries, the Octave of Prayer for Christian Unity commences seven days before the Feast of the Conversion of Saint Paul (January 25). A series of themes is usually approved by the Ordinary and episcopal conference or by an ecumenical body to promote prayers for specific intentions on each day of this non-liturgical octave. The Mass for Christian Unity should be celebrated when the day permits. Ecumenical forms of worship and meetings may appropriately include welcoming other Christians to take part in a festive celebration of the Liturgy of the Hours.

O little Child, lying in a manger, through a star, heaven has called and led the Magi to you; these first fruits of the Gentiles are astonished to see neither thrones nor scepters but extreme poverty. What, indeed, is lower than a cave or humbler than swaddling clothes? Yet in them the splendor of your divinity shone forth resplendently. Glory to you, O Lord!

— The Byzantine *Hypacoi* of Christmas

3.

Presentation of the Lord

64. In obedience to the Old Law, the Lord Jesus, the first-born, was presented in the Temple by his Blessed Mother and his foster father. This is another "epiphany" celebration insofar as the Christ Child is revealed as the Messiah through the canticle and words of Simeon and the testimony of Anna the prophetess. Christ is the light of the nations, hence the blessing and procession of candles on this day. In the Middle Ages this feast of the Purification of the Blessed Virgin Mary, or "Candlemas", was of great importance.[1]

65. The specific liturgy of this Candlemas feast, the blessing of candles, is not as widely celebrated as it should be, except of course whenever February 2 falls on a Sunday and thus takes precedence. There are two ways of celebrating the ceremony, either the *Procession*, which begins at a "gathering place" outside the church, or the *Solemn Entrance*, celebrated within the church.

Immediate Preparations

66. *Altar*: six or four candles lit, white antependium.

67. *Ambo*: Lectionary, marked for the readings, white antependium.

---

[1] See Eamon Duffy, *The Stripping of the Altars, Traditional Religion in England 1400–1580* (New Haven, Conn.: Yale University Press, 1992), pp. 15–22.

68. *Chair*: a white chasuble, if the celebrant wears a white cope for the procession.

69. *Credence table*: the usual requirements for Mass.

70. *Table of gifts*: bread, wine and water for the procession of gifts.

71. *Sacristy*: white eucharistic vestments for the celebrant (concelebrants) and deacon(s) or a white cope for the celebrant; hand candles for clergy and servers who are not carrying another object; Book of the Gospels, marked; a vessel of holy water and sprinkler.

72. *Gathering place (or porch or narthex, etc., for the Solemn Entrance)*: according to local custom, candles to be used in the church during the year are arranged on a table, covered with a cloth; a microphone, if necessary.

First Form: Procession

73. At the gathering place, the ushers or servers distribute hand candles to the faithful before the blessing and procession, but the candles remain unlit at this stage. (In some places the faithful bring their own candles to the church.) The celebrant and servers leave the sacristy and go in procession to the gathering place or chapel where candles will be blessed.[2] The deacon carries the Book of the Gospels. All those who are not carrying another object carry unlit candles. The M.C. or a server brings the celebrant's hand candle. A server carries the vessel of holy water and sprinkler.

74. Just as they arrive at the gathering place, all the hand candles are lit while the antiphon "The Lord will come with mighty

---

[2] Cf. MR, *Presentation of the Lord*, nos. 1–2. If the procession goes outdoors, glass protectors will be needed for the two processional candles.

power" or a suitable hymn is sung. Ushers and servers assist the faithful.[3] Then, facing the people and assisted by the book bearer, the celebrant says "+ In the name of the Father . . ." and greets the people as he would at the beginning of Mass. He introduces the rite using the formula provided or some other words. Alternatively, the deacon or a concelebrant may introduce the rite. If the deacon introduces the rite, a lector or server takes the Book of the Gospels and holds it while the deacon or concelebrant addresses the faithful and carries out any other duties before the procession begins.

75. Extending his hands, the celebrant sings or says the prayer of blessing and makes the sign of the cross over the candles carried by the assembly as well as over any other candles arranged on a table nearby. A server presents the holy water vessel to him, and he sprinkles the candles—in practice those who are holding them. If he has to walk among the faithful, the deacon, M.C. or a server holds back the right side of the cope to free his hand during the sprinkling.

76. The thurifer approaches and incense is blessed as usual; the thurifer bows and goes to a position to lead the procession with the cross bearer and candle bearers. The deacon or M.C. hands the celebrant his candle. The deacon, a concelebrant or, lacking either, the celebrant himself sings or says, "Let us go in peace to meet the Lord", and the procession begins. Moving at a dignified pace, the procession follows this order: thurifer, cross bearer, candle bearers, choir and/or cantors, clergy in choir dress, deacon or lector carrying the Book of the Gospels, concelebrants, celebrant (with a second deacon) and the faithful. Ushers should supervise the procession and maintain due order.

---

[3] The hand candles are usually initially lit from the two processional candles. Tapers may be useful to facilitate the process.

77. During the procession either the antiphon "Christ is the light of the nations . . ." with the canticle Nunc Dimittis or an appropriate hymn is sung. If the celebrant wears a cope, two deacons, or the deacon and M.C., or two servers may hold it back during the procession. It is assumed that this procession takes a long route, outside or, even if necessary, inside the church. Therefore the entrance antiphon or hymn is only sung once the procession either enters the church or begins to move down the aisle to the sanctuary. The faithful go to their places at this stage, ushers guiding them if necessary.

78. On arriving at the sanctuary, the servers go to their usual places. The deacon puts the Book of the Gospels on the altar and waits there. The celebrant comes before the altar; he hands his candle to the M.C. or a server (who extinguishes it and takes it to the credence table) and then genuflects or bows. He goes to the altar, and (with the deacon[s]) he kisses it. The altar is incensed as usual.[4] More incense may be put in the thurible by a server just before the incensation of the altar. Then the celebrant goes to the chair. If the cope has been worn, it is now removed and replaced by the chasuble. The deacon, M.C. or a server assists the celebrant.[5] Then the celebrant intones the Gloria.[6] After the Gloria the celebrant sings or says the Opening Prayer as usual, and the Liturgy of the Word follows. Strictly speaking, candles should be extinguished at the conclusion of the procession, but it would seem more convenient, and seemly,

---

[4] If the celebrant wears a cope, the deacon(s), deacon and M.C., concelebrants, or the M.C. alone should hold it back to free his arms during the incensation, as is customary at Solemn Vespers; see CMRR, no. 734.

[5] A server should take the cope back to the sacristy.

[6] CB, no. 247, also allows for the cope to be removed and replaced by the chasuble immediately on arriving before the altar, but this seems fussy and destroys the flow of the ceremony.

for all who carried candles in the procession to extinguish them only after the Opening Prayer.[7] A server collects the candles of those who assist in the sanctuary and takes them to the credence table or the sacristy.

The Bishop Presides on the Presentation of the Lord

79. The bishop wears the cope or chasuble and the ornate miter, and he carries the crozier. However, because he carries a hand candle during the procession, the crozier bearer walks directly in front of him carrying the crozier within the vimpa.[8] The book bearer and miter bearer follow him, preceding the faithful in the procession. If the cope has been worn, it is replaced by the chasuble (and pontifical dalmatic, if worn) after the incensation of the altar.

80. Because of the oblative and revelatory symbolism of the Temple offering of the Child Jesus, this day is observed as a distinctive celebration for all consecrated religious men and women in the Church. Following the example given by the Pope in Rome, in each diocese religious men and women and others in vows should be welcomed to the cathedral to take part in the procession and to share with their bishop in the celebration of the Eucharist.

Second Form: Solemn Entrance

81. The solemn entrance takes place within the church and should be chosen only when it is not possible to have a procession. Before the ceremony, the ushers or servers distribute hand candles to the faithful, either as they enter the

---

[7] This would be in harmony with the Palm Sunday Procession, which concludes with the Opening Prayer; cf. MR, Holy Week, *Passion Sunday*.

[8] Cf. CB, no. 246.

church or once they have gone to their seats, but the candles remain unlit at this stage.

82. The celebrant and servers, and some representatives of the faithful with unlit candles, go in procession to a suitable place, usually the narthex, a porch or an area just inside the main door. If possible this procession should come from the sacristy without going through the church. Just as the procession arrives at this place all the hand candles are lit while the antiphon "The Lord will come with mighty power . . ." or a suitable hymn is sung. Ushers and servers assist the faithful, who should also be encouraged to turn to face the place where the blessing will be celebrated. The blessing and preparations for the procession follow exactly as set out above. In the procession through the church, the representatives of the faithful follow the celebrant, carrying their candles. They go to their places when the celebrant enters the sanctuary.

83. However, if the procession goes directly to the altar from the place where candles were blessed, the antiphon and Nunc Dimittis or the hymn may well replace the entrance antiphon or entrance hymn. Another possibility would be for the solemn entrance to take the form of a longer procession around the interior of the church, with the appropriate antiphon, etc., and for the entrance antiphon or hymn to begin only when the procession begins to move down the main aisle towards the altar.[9] Once the celebrant and servers have arrived at the sanctuary, the Mass begins as described above.

---

[9] In churches where the solemn procession outdoors would take place under normal circumstances, this alternative would be a good way of celebrating the rite during inclement weather.

84. If the candles that will be used in the church during the year have also been blessed, these should be brought to the sacristy by the sacristan(s) immediately after the procession or solemn entrance.[10] This occasion may also serve as a reminder to order the new Easter candle for the current year. It is customary for the faithful to take their blessed candles home after the Mass, so they can be used within the prayer life of the domestic church.

Saint Blaise, Bishop and Martyr, February 3

85. On the day after the Presentation of Our Lord, the memorial of Saint Blaise, it is customary in many places to bless the throats of the faithful with two candles tied together with a red ribbon to form a cross. The candles are privately blessed with the prayer provided in the *Book of Blessings* or in the preconciliar *Roman Ritual,* title IX, chapter III. The rite of the blessing of throats may take place before or after Mass.

86. The priest or deacon places the candles around the throat of whoever seeks the blessing, using the formula: "Through the intercession of Saint Blaise, bishop and martyr, may God deliver you free from every disease of the throat, and from every other disease. In the name of the Father and of the Son, + and of the Holy Spirit. ℟. Amen." Because the celebrant makes the sign of the cross with his right hand, it is best to apply the candles with both hands. Then the celebrant withdraws his right hand to make the sign of the cross, while continuing to hold the candles in place with his left hand. For the convenience of the celebrant the formula should be printed on a small card, attached to the candles.

---

[10] A stock of good quality candles purchased a year in advance will be found to burn better.

The World Day of the Sick, February 11

87. The memorial of Our Lady of Lourdes, February 11, was proclaimed the World Day of the Sick by Pope John Paul II. Therefore, it would be appropriate to celebrate the Sacrament of the Anointing of the Sick on that day during a Mass or Liturgy of the Word.[11]

> Let us then turn this Festival to account by taking it as the Memorial-day of His visitations. Let us from the events it celebrates, lay up deep in our hearts the recollection, how mysteriously little things are in this world connected with great; how single moments, improved or wasted, are the salvation or ruin of all-important interests. Let us bear the thought upon us, when we come to worship in God's House, that any such season of service may, for what we know, be wonderfully connected with some ancient purpose of His, announced before we were born, and may have its determinate bearing on our eternal welfare; let us fear to miss the Saviour, while Simeon and Anna find Him.
>
> — Ven. John Henry Cardinal Newman, "Secrecy and Suddenness of Divine Visitations (The Feast of the Purification of the Blessed Virgin)", *Parochial and Plain Sermons*

---

[11] The Sacrament of the Anointing of the Sick is only to be given to "those of the faithful whose health is *seriously* impaired by sickness or old age", RR, *Pastoral Care of the Sick*, Introduction, 8. This Sacrament must not be given indiscriminately to all who take part in Masses for the sick on February 11 and other occasions.

4.

Lent

88. The distinctive English word "Lent" is derived from the Anglo-Saxon word for "spring", which appropriately coincides with the great forty-day fast, common to both East and West at least since the fourth century. Notwithstanding the fact that autumn occurs at this time in the Southern Hemisphere, the English word has the advantage over the Latin words based on "quadraginta" or "forty" because it calls to mind the new life, growth, hope and change that should characterize this time of prayer, penance and conversion, this season of initiation into the grace life of the Church.

89. In these forty days, Mother Church vests herself simply in violet. Her sacred halls are bare, and much of her gracious music is muted. Flowers at her altars and shrines are set aside, and, at the end of the season, the lamps will be extinguished, the bells will fall silent and her altars will be stripped. But this is her true springtime, when her children grow in grace, in ways often imperceptible, subtle and varied. Lent thus reminds us that the great graces are given by God, not when our senses perceive them or when our hearts are full of consolations, but in the silence and the stillness of "the night".

90. A certain austerity should thus characterize the setting of the Lenten liturgy. Simpler candlesticks may well be placed on or around the altar. Flowers are not used to adorn the altar from Ash Wednesday until the Gloria at the Easter Vigil, except for Lætare Sunday, solemnities and feast days.[1] It would be best to exclude them entirely from the church, even at popular shrines, during the whole penitential season. The organ and other instruments are to be used only to sustain singing. The Te Deum and the Gloria are sung or said on solemnities or feasts, but not on the Sundays of Lent. "Alleluia" is never sung or said on any day until the Easter Vigil, and hymns that include this praise should be excluded.

91. During Lent, an appropriate Mass for various needs and occasions may only be celebrated when there is some genuine need or pastoral advantage.[2] Votive Masses and daily Masses for the dead are prohibited.[3] Because the weekdays of Lent take precedence, the memorials of saints are celebrated in a reduced way, as follows: (a) the Opening Prayer at Mass may be that of the saint, if the saint is to be found in the General Roman Calendar, but the Mass is of the day and violet vestments are worn;[4] (b) after the final prayer at Lauds and Vespers, the antiphon and the prayer of the saint are added; (c) at the Office of Readings, after the prescribed second reading and its responsory, the reading of the saint, its responsory and the prayer of the saint are added.[5] Solemnities and feasts are not modified, except for the suppression of the Alleluia.

---

[1] Cf. GIRM, no. 305; CB, nos. 48, 252. "On the altar" would include the whole sanctuary. But holy water stoups are not emptied until after the Mass of the Lord's Supper on Holy Thursday. Filling them with "desert sand" during Lent is modern nonsense.

[2] Cf. GIRM, no. 374.

[3] Cf. GIRM, no. 381.

[4] Cf. GIRM, no. 355 a.

[5] Cf. *Principles and Norms for the Liturgy of the Hours*, nos. 237–39.

92. The public celebration of the sacraments in Lent should be characterized by a certain restraint. Those who seek to be married during Lent should be advised to take account of the penitential season and thus accept a limitation of outward signs of solemnity and festivity.[6]

93. During Lent the Sacrament of Penance should be readily available, and pastors should ensure that ample opportunity is offered for confessions according to the First Rite of Reconciliation. Where possible, the priests in a deanery or region should come together for celebrations of the Second Rite of Reconciliation.[7] This is also a season for focused preaching at weekday Mass and other celebrations.[8]

Ash Wednesday

94. At the beginning of Lent, on Ash Wednesday, ashes are blessed during Mass, after the homily. The blessed ashes are then "imposed" on the faithful as a sign of conversion, penance, fasting and human mortality. The ashes are blessed at least during the first Mass of the day, but they may also be imposed during all the Masses of the day, after the homily, and even outside the time of Mass to meet the needs of the faithful.[9] Priests or deacons normally impart this sacramen-

---

[6] Cf. *Roman Ritual* (henceforth RR), *Rite of Marriage*, no. 32. In practice this means that, whenever possible, marriages during Lent should be discouraged. At Lenten celebrations of marriage, flowers could be used in moderation, but removed after the celebration.

[7] Cf. CB, no. 251; *Circular Letter concerning the Preparation and Celebration of the Easter Feasts* (henceforth CLE), Congregation for Divine Worship, 1988, no. 15. The norms in this *Circular Letter* have been included in the third edition of the Roman Missal.

[8] Cf. CLE, no. 13.

[9] It seems that more ashes may be blessed at later Masses, for a good pastoral reason. Ashes are blessed outside Mass within the celebration of the Liturgy of the Word for the day; cf. MR, end note to Ash Wednesday.

tal, but instituted acolytes, other extraordinary ministers or designated lay people may be delegated to impart ashes, if the bishop judges that this is necessary. The ashes are made from the palms used at the previous Passion Sunday ceremonies.[10] These ashes should be reduced to powder and then placed in bowls.[11]

Immediate Preparations

95. *Altar*: two or four candles, violet antependium.

96. *Ambo*: Lectionary, marked, violet antependium.

97. *Chair*: Missal or book of the chair, a small table, preferably covered with violet fabric, may be set up in front of or near the chair with the bowl(s) of ashes to be blessed.

98. *Credence table*: as well as the usual requirements for Mass: (bowl[s] of ashes to be blessed, if a table is not set up near the chair) the vessel containing holy water with the sprinkler; bowl(s) of warm water, soap and towel(s) for cleansing the fingers of the celebrant and others who impose ashes.

99. *Table of gifts*: bread, wine and water for the procession of gifts.

100. *Sacristy*: Violet eucharistic vestments for the celebrant (concelebrants) and deacon(s); Book of the Gospels, marked. Other clergy who impose ashes wear an alb or cassock and surplice and a violet stole.

---

[10] Cf. MR, *Ash Wednesday*. Obviously this requirement would be waived if there were not enough palms left to provide ashes. The sacristan burns the palms or other dried foliage in a metal vessel, carefully retrieves the ash and then prepares it for blessing by breaking it down into a powder.

[11] In some places, especially in a warmer climate, water is added to the ashes to make a paste that will leave a mark on the forehead.

101. After the entrance procession (and the incensation of the altar) the Mass begins as usual with the sign of the cross and greeting, but the Penitential Rite is omitted, thus the celebrant sings or says "Let us pray" and the Opening Prayer, and the Liturgy of the Word follows. After the homily, all stand. If a small table was not set up in front of or near the chair, the bowls of ashes may be brought from the credence table and held before the celebrant by servers. Directed by the M.C., a server brings the holy water vessel from the credence table. At the chair, facing the people and assisted by the book bearer, the celebrant introduces the rite of blessing, using the formula provided or some other words. Extending his hands, he sings or says either of the prayers of blessing and makes the sign of the cross over the ashes. A server presents the holy water vessel to him, and he sprinkles the ashes in silence.

102. The deacon or a concelebrant or another priest sprinkles ashes on the celebrant's head, while he bows, using either of the formulae: "Turn away . . ." or "Remember. . . ." If there is no other priest or a deacon present, the celebrant imposes the ashes on himself. Then the celebrant imposes ashes on the deacon(s), concelebrants, clergy in choir, the servers and other members of the faithful, saying either: "Turn away . . ." or "Remember. . . ."[12] To impose ashes it is customary to take the ashes with the thumb and mark the forehead with the sign of the cross. However, ashes may be sprinkled in the form of a cross on the crown of the head of men in major Orders, while they bow. The faithful come to receive blessed ashes at the place where they usually receive Communion, standing or kneeling, according to local

---

[12] The deacon or a server may hold the bowl of ashes while the celebrant imposes them on himself and on others, but it may be more convenient for him to hold it himself.

custom.[13] As noted, where necessary, the deacon, concelebrants, other priests or deacons and, where permitted by the bishop, delegated laity may also impose ashes. During the imposition the antiphons or appropriate penitential hymns are sung.

103.   After the imposition, the celebrant gives the bowl of ashes to the M.C. or a server (who takes it to the credence table). He bows or genuflects and returns to the chair and sits. Servers bring the water, soap and towel to cleanse his hands. Others who imposed ashes take the bowls of ashes to the credence table and cleanse their hands there. Then the celebrant stands, and, assisted by the book bearer, he introduces the General Intercessions, which conclude the rite. The Creed is omitted. Mass follows as usual, with the Fourth Preface for Lent.

The Bishop Presides on Ash Wednesday

104.   The bishop wears the simple miter, and he carries the crozier. After the homily, the miter is removed, and he blesses the ashes, standing at the cathedra as described above. Then the M.C. or deacon removes the skullcap, and a concelebrant or deacon[14] imposes ashes on him at the cathedra, while he bows. Then he receives the skullcap and miter, and, seated or standing at the cathedra, he imposes ashes on deacon(s), concelebrants, canons and clergy in choir and the servers.[15] He then goes to the customary place and imposes ashes on the faithful, assisted by the other clergy.

---

[13] As this is a penitential act, kneeling may well be preferred.

[14] It may be customary for the senior-ranking prelate present to impose ashes on the bishop, that is, the dean or administrator of the cathedral or a senior canon.

[15] Cf. CB, nos. 256–58. The M.C. supervises an orderly procession to the cathedra so those within the sanctuary can receive ashes from the bishop.

He returns to the cathedra and sits while two servers bring the pontifical ewer and basin, soap and a towel to cleanse his hands. The miter is removed, and he stands to lead the General Intercessions. Mass follows as described above.

Blessing of Ashes outside of Mass

105. Where Mass cannot be celebrated, the rite of blessing and imposition of ashes may take place within a Liturgy of the Word, using the readings provided for the day.[16] This celebration concludes with the General Intercessions and a blessing. Outside the time of Mass, ashes may be imposed according to pastoral need. It may also be customary to take blessed ashes to those confined at home or in hospitals or rest homes, usually within the context of eucharistic ministry to the sick. Blessed ashes that are left over are mixed with water and poured into the sacrarium or down the drain of the font or into the garden.

Sundays in Lent

106. The Sundays in Lent rank as solemnities, although the Gloria is not sung or said. These Sundays have their own distinctive pattern, based on their relationship to the rites of Christian Initiation, the readings provided for each Sunday in the three cycles of the Roman Lectionary and the way each Sunday steadily leads the faithful towards Holy Week and the great Triduum. The readings provided in cycle A for the Third, Fourth and Fifth Sundays are related to the rites of Christian Initiation and can be read in other years, especially if there are catechumens in the community.[17] The third edition of the Roman Missal provides proper prefaces

---

[16] Cf. MR, *Ash Wednesday.*
[17] Cf. CLE, no. 24.

for the Sundays in Lent, and a Prayer over the people before the blessing for all Lenten Masses.

107. Whether or not the rite of election of catechumens is celebrated on the First Sunday in Lent, the principal Mass should include some distinctive elements, such as a solemn entrance procession during which the Litany of the Saints is chanted.[18] Such a procession should move slowly around the interior of the church, if necessary several times, so as to approach the sanctuary only when most of the Litany has been sung. It should be led by the thurifer, cross bearer and candle bearers. It would be appropriate for Lenten banners to be carried in the procession. The cantors and/or choir either take part in the procession or sing from their own place, according to local custom. The names of the patron saint, the founder of the order or congregation, local saints, etc., may be inserted at the appropriate place in the Litany.

108. On the Fourth Sunday in Lent (Lætare Sunday), rose-colored vestments may be used, and the rule restricting flowers and musical instruments may be relaxed somewhat on a day when a sense of joyful anticipation is evident.[19] Passiontide is the deeper time of Lent, beginning with the First Vespers of the Fifth Sunday in Lent. But this is no longer called "Passion Sunday", because that title is now reserved for Palm Sunday to mark the beginning of Holy Week. The First Preface of the Passion is used during the fifth week of Lent.

---

[18] Cf. CB, no. 261; CLE, no. 23.
[19] Cf. CB, no. 252; CLE, no. 25.

Rites of Christian Initiation

109. The solemn rites of Christian Initiation span the season of
Lent, culminating in the Baptism and Confirmation of the
elect during the solemn Easter Vigil. The catechumens enter the ranks of the elect at the beginning of Lent, through
the rite of election and enrollment of names, which may be
celebrated during Mass on the First Sunday of Lent. Then
begins the period of enlightenment or purification or illumi-
nation. Together with their godparents, the elect gather for
the scrutinies that mark specific stages of their spiritual journey towards full sacramental incorporation into the Body
of Christ. The first, second and third scrutiny are celebrated respectively on the Third, Fourth and Fifth Sundays in
Lent. Unless the rites have already taken place during the
catechumenate, the presentation of the Profession of Faith
and the Lord's Prayer are celebrated in the weeks that follow the Third and Fourth Sundays of Lent.

110. Other rites such as the recitation of the Profession of Faith,
the ephphetha, choosing a Christian name and the anointing
with the Oil of Catechumens are celebrated according to
the directives of the episcopal conference and local custom,
usually in the last weeks of Lent or in Holy Week as preparation for Baptism during the Easter Vigil. Therefore the
anointing with the Oil of Catechumens and the recitation
of the Creed may serve as a rite of immediate preparation
on Holy Saturday.

111. In the particular Church, the bishop is to take a special interest in supervising the catechumenate in its final stages
leading to the great sacraments of Christian Initiation. He
should endeavor to be involved in the major celebrations
of the various rites leading to the Easter Vigil itself, and

it would be appropriate, where possible, to celebrate these rites in the cathedral. The bishop should celebrate the rite of election in the cathedral, or in some other appropriate church, during Mass on the First Sunday in Lent.[20] At the same time the penitential focus of the season is maintained through other liturgical celebrations where the bishop himself presides.

Stational Celebrations in Lent

112. In Rome, an ancient Lenten tradition is the visit of the Pope to preside over penitential liturgical assemblies in the "stational churches" and in other places. In the Roman Missal, this custom is recommended for all the other particular Churches in communion with the Church of Rome.[21] These celebrations take place when the bishop visits key places in his diocese, such as the tombs of saints, principal churches or shrines in the city or elsewhere, or frequently visited places of pilgrimage. These Lenten assemblies are celebrated on Sundays or weekdays, according to pastoral need, in parish churches or places of pilgrimage.[22]

113. Each Lenten liturgical assembly may begin with a solemn penitential procession, led by the bishop. He wears a violet cope or violet eucharistic vestments and the simple miter, and he carries the crozier. If possible, the procession begins at a designated gathering place where the faithful assemble, outside the church, that is, at another church, chapel or suitable place.[23] Preceded by the thurifer, cross bearer,

---

[20] Cf. CB, nos. 408–10.

[21] Cf. MR, introductory note 1 at the beginning of the Lenten Season.

[22] Cf. CB, no. 260. According to pastoral need, the Ordinary may invite his auxiliary bishops to preside over such celebrations.

[23] As with other liturgical processions, due to weather or social factors, the procession may have to take place within the church.

candle bearers, robed choir, other servers, clergy in choir dress and vested concelebrants, the bishop comes from the sacristy to this place, while a suitable hymn is sung. He gives the crozier and miter to a server and greets the people. The bishop, a concelebrant or deacon introduces the celebration. Attended by the book bearer, the bishop says an opening prayer, with hands extended, on the mystery of the holy Cross or for the remission of sins or for the Church, especially the particular Church, or one of the prayers over the people provided in the Roman Missal. Then he receives the miter, and he may prepare and bless incense. The deacon or, lacking a deacon, a concelebrant sings or says, "Let us go forth in peace", and the procession begins to move towards the church.

114. During the procession, the Litany of the Saints is sung, led by the cantor(s) or the choir. The names of the patron saint, the founder of the order or congregation, local saints, etc., may be inserted at the appropriate place in the Litany. On arrival at the sanctuary, Mass begins with the incensation of the altar. The bishop then goes to the chair, removes the cope and puts on the chasuble. The opening rites are omitted, and the Kyrie may be omitted. The bishop sings or says the Opening Prayer, and Mass continues according to the day.[24]

115. This penitential procession may also precede a celebration of the word of God or one of the penitential services for Lent provided in appendix 2 of the *Rite of Penance*.[25] It would seem suitable also to have such a procession before a major celebration of the Second Rite of Reconciliation presided over by the bishop. During Lent, due provision should be

---

[24] Cf. CB, no. 261.

[25] Cf. CB, no. 262, and see nos. 224–26 and 640–43 for a description of such rites.

made for easier access to the Sacrament of Penance, especially on occasions when the faithful gather for processions or devotions. The celebration of the Sacrament of Penance should be evident from its solemn liturgical form, according to the Second Rite of Reconciliation.[26]

Solemnities during Lent

116. The Solemnity of Saint Joseph, March 19, and the Solemnity of the Annunciation of the Lord, March 25, always fall during Lent. If they coincide with a Sunday, they are celebrated on the following day. If they fall from Palm Sunday to Easter Day, they are usually postponed until the Monday after the Second Sunday of Easter. On March 25, as at Christmas, during the Creed, all kneel at the words "by the power of the Holy Spirit . . . man".[27] The celebrant and deacon(s) may kneel before the altar.

The Way of the Cross

117. The devotion that is most appropriate in Lent and Holy Week is the symbolic re-enactment of Our Lord's "Via Dolorosa" in Jerusalem. The Way of the Cross or "Stations of the Cross" gradually spread through the Counter-Reformation Church and today remains one of the most popular public or private devotions to the Sacred Passion of Our Lord. It is commended as particularly appropriate in Lent, as it harmonizes with the season.[28] Traditionally, the fourteen "stations" are crosses set up inside the nave or in another area within or even outside the church. At each cross and the image that customarily accompanies it, the

---

[26] Cf. CB, no. 251.
[27] Cf. MR, propers for the Annunciation.
[28] Cf. CLE, no. 20.

clergy and faithful pause in procession to recall the saving events of the Passion and death of Our Redeemer.

118. This devotion should be a real procession, moving from station to station. In churches where the stations are grouped together in one small area, or normally set up in a side chapel, they could well be rearranged around the main body of the church during Lent, not only for a better public celebration of the Way of the Cross but also to encourage private devotion at this time.

119. The celebrant is assisted by a cross bearer, two candle bearers and perhaps a book bearer. According to the Roman custom, the cross carried may be a large bare wooden cross, painted black or red, and the candles may be two of the "torches" used at Solemn Mass. A priest or deacon wears an alb, or cassock and surplice, and a violet or red stole.[29] A violet or red cope may be worn for a solemn celebration or if the devotion is part of a longer para-liturgy. It is customary to sing the verses of the "Stabat Mater" or another appropriate hymn while proceeding from station to station, hence a choir greatly enhances participation.

120. Two candles may be lit at the main altar. A microphone should be used in a large church.[30] The cross bearer and candle bearers lead the celebrant to the sanctuary. If he kneels for an opening prayer, they remain standing. During the first verse of the hymn they go to the first station. If, because of the large numbers present, it is not convenient for all the faithful to move from station to station, some representatives of the faithful may join in the procession.[31]

---

[29] Red is used on Palm Sunday and Good Friday.

[30] The celebrant should use a cordless or portable microphone while speaking at each station.

[31] When no servers are available, some of the faithful may well carry the cross and candles.

It is customary for the cross bearer and candle bearers to stand with their backs to each station, facing the celebrant and the faithful. If the celebrant recites the verse: "We adore you, O Christ . . .", the cross bearer and candle bearers remain standing while the celebrant and faithful genuflect. To focus on the meaning of each station, the celebrant usually remains facing the station while leading whatever prayers and points for meditation have been chosen.

121. After the last station, the servers lead the celebrant back to the sanctuary for the final prayers. During these prayers before the altar (a) the cross bearer stands at the center, flanked by the candle bearers, all facing the people, with the celebrant in front of them facing the cross, or (b) the celebrant faces the altar while the cross bearer and candle bearers stand behind him, also facing the altar. If the celebrant and faithful kneel for the prayers, the servers remain standing. At the conclusion of the devotion, the celebrant may follow the Roman custom of taking the wooden cross in his hands and blessing the people with it; he makes the sign of the cross with it, saying "May the blessing of almighty God. . . ." The devotion is best concluded in silence, as the celebrant and servers return to the sacristy.

122. The Way of the Cross offers some scope for adaptation. For example, different speakers or actors might dramatize the events, and the devotion can be enriched by drawing on Scripture readings, good music, poetry and sacred silence. While undue theatricality should be avoided, dramatic use of light and darkness may help the faithful to focus on each event of the journey of the Lord. If the devotion is significantly adapted, the celebrant should only lead the essential prayers. However, the events should be allowed to speak for themselves and not become heavy either with didacticism (by way of a running commentary) or sentimentalism. The

Way of the Cross is also easy to adapt for the spiritual needs of children. This applies even to the smallest ones, but it may be best to take them through a very simple and brief Way of the Cross in a less formal way, preferably in small groups.

123. Since the Second Vatican Council, some alternative sets of the stations have been proposed, duly authorized, and even set up in a few churches. Based on earlier forms of the Way of the Cross, these stations adhere to the Sacred Scriptures and eliminate incidents that are not found there.[32] However, because these stations usually conclude rather suddenly with the Resurrection, they may seem inappropriate during Lent. Under normal circumstances, as a Lenten devotion, it would seem pastorally wise to retain the Way of the Cross that is familiar to the faithful.

Veiling Crosses and Images

124. As already noted, the First Preface of the Passion is used during the Fifth Week of Lent, marking the beginning of the last phase of Lent, traditionally known as Passiontide. The custom of veiling crosses and images in these last two weeks of Lent has much to commend it in terms of religious psychology, because it helps us to concentrate on the great essentials of Christ's work of Redemption. The episcopal conference decides whether this should be obligatory within its territory,[33] but any pastor may choose to restore

---

[32] At first sight this seems praiseworthy, but if anyone were to *insist* on using only these scriptural stations, rejecting the set that is customary, such an attitude would be more in tune with the spirit of the condemned Jansenist Synod of Pistoia (1786) than with the broader pastoral mind of the postconciliar Church. However, these new stations can be of value for ecumenical acts of worship during Lent.

[33] Cf. MR, *Fifth Sunday of Lent*; CLE, no. 26.

or maintain this wise practice in his own parish. The violet veils should preferably be made of a plain light fabric, without any decoration. The Stations of the Cross and images in stained-glass windows are never veiled. Crosses and images are veiled before the First Vespers or vigil Mass of the Fifth Sunday in Lent. Crosses are unveiled after the Good Friday ceremonies. All other images are unveiled, without any ceremony, just before the Easter Vigil begins.

Beloved, here is the way where we found our salvation, Jesus Christ, the High Priest offering our gifts, patron and help in our weakness. Through him we look directly into the heavens above. Through him we see the reflection of the flawless and transcendent countenance of God. Through him were opened the eyes of our heart. Through him our dull and darkened mind shoots up into light. Through him the Master was pleased to let us taste a knowledge that never fades away, for, "He reflects the glory of God . . . having become as much superior to angels as the name he has obtained is more excellent than theirs . . ." (Hebrews 1:3–4).

— Pope Saint Clement I, *Letter to the Corinthians*, 36.

5.

Passion (Palm) Sunday and Holy Week

Passion (Palm) Sunday

125. Holy Week begins with Passion Sunday, more popularly known as Palm Sunday, because this day first celebrates the regal entrance of Our Lord into Jerusalem, where he will face his bitter Passion for us sinners. The re-enactment of his entry into the Holy City is expressed through the sacramental of blessed palm or olive branches, carried by the "children of the Hebrews". The "palms" may literally be portions of a type of palm or olive branches or fronds or leaves taken from a local tree. In some places it is customary to use small crosses woven of palm fronds.

126. The procession in honor of Christ the King is to be prepared and celebrated to bring out its spiritual significance in the lives of the faithful.[1] It is only the first liturgical procession of a series of processions that make up the major distinctive acts in the celebration of Holy Week and the Easter Triduum: the procession of palms, the procession of the Holy Oils, the Eucharistic Procession on Holy Thursday, the procession of the Veneration of the Cross and bringing in the Eucharist on Good Friday, the procession of light and the baptismal processions at the Easter Vigil. These movements should all be carried out reverently and

---

[1] Cf. CLE, no. 29.

precisely, and catechesis on each of these sacred and symbolic "movements" should be part of the liturgical teaching at this time.

127. On Palm Sunday there are three forms of celebrating the Commemoration of the Lord's Entrance into Jerusalem: (1) the procession, (2) the solemn entrance or (3) the simple entrance. The first form is to be preferred, even if there is no deacon and only several servers.

128. Everything is prepared for a Solemn Mass, with deacon(s), (concelebrants and) M.C. and the full complement of servers: cross and candle bearers, thurifer(s), book bearer, two, four or six torch bearers. The Passion narrative should be sung or read in the traditional way by three persons taking the parts of Christ, the narrator and the people. Three vested deacons or the celebrant and deacons or skilled lectors proclaim the Passion. If only lectors are available, the part of Christ is read by the priest.[2] Where the procession and Mass take a simpler form, an M.C. should direct the ceremonies and a server or servers act as the book bearer and the cross bearer. Another server acts as thurifer during the procession, and members of the faithful should carry palms. The celebrant and skilled lectors proclaim the Passion.

Immediate Preparations for the
First Form: the Procession

129. *Altar*: six or four candles lit, (red antependium); the altar crucifix may be veiled in red.

130. *Ambo*: the Lectionary, marked, red antependium, but no antependium if the Passion is to be read here. Three bare

---

[2] Cf. CLE, no. 33.

matching lecterns are set up at the center of the sanctuary just before the Passion is read, or two bare lecterns may be placed on each side of the bare ambo for the other readers of the Passion, unless the ambo is wide enough for three people.

131.   *Chair*: a red chasuble, if the celebrant wears a cope for the procession.

132.   *Credence table*: the usual requirements for Mass, a salver or tray for palms.

133.   *Table of gifts*: bread, wine and water for the procession of gifts.

134.   *Sacristy*: red eucharistic vestments for the celebrant (concelebrants) and deacon(s), or a red cope for the celebrant; palms for clergy and servers who are not carrying another object; Book of the Gospels, marked; Missal or order of Holy Week; the processional cross adorned with palms; a vessel of holy water and sprinkler; palms for those who do not carry another object. For those who read the Passion: albs and red stoles, if they are deacons, or albs, if they are laity.

135.   *Gathering place*: a lectern (with a red antependium); palms to be distributed; a microphone, if necessary.

The Procession

136.   At the gathering place, the ushers or servers distribute palms to the faithful before the clergy and servers arrive for the blessing, Gospel and procession. Led by the thurifer, cross bearer and candle bearers, the celebrant, clergy and servers leave the sacristy and go to the gathering place, following

the same order of procession as for a Solemn Mass.[3] The deacon carries the Book of the Gospels. The vested deacons who will read the Passion follow him, carrying the books of the Passion.[4] Laity in albs who will read the Passion precede him, carrying the books of the Passion. All those who are not carrying another object carry a palm. The M.C. or a server brings the celebrant's palm. The book bearer brings the Missal or order of Holy Week. Another server carries the vessel of holy water and sprinkler.

137. Just as they arrive at the gathering place, the antiphon "Hosanna to the Son of David . . ." or a suitable hymn is sung. Directed by the M.C., the thurifer, cross bearer and candle bearers take a position behind or near the place where the celebrant will stand. The deacon (or a concelebrant or lector, if no deacon is present) places the Book of the Gospels on the lectern. Then, facing the people and assisted by the book bearer, the celebrant says "+ In the name of the Father . . ." and greets the people as at the beginning of Mass. He introduces the rite using the formula provided or some other words. Alternatively, the deacon or a concelebrant may introduce the rite. Extending his hands, the celebrant sings or says the prayer of blessing and, if the first alternative blessing is chosen, he makes the sign of the cross over the palms carried by the assembly. A server presents the holy water vessel to him, and he sprinkles the palms (in practice those who are holding them). If he has to walk among the faithful, the deacon, M.C. or a server may hold back the right side of the cope to free his hand during the sprinkling.

---

[3] See CMRR, appendix 11, diagram 2, Solemn Mass, or diagram 5, Solemn Pontifical Mass.

[4] Following the same order as for the procession of palms, cf. CB, no. 270, that is, unless these deacons must also act as assistant deacons to the bishop, in which case they walk on each side of him.

138. Preparations are now made for the reading of the Gospel account of Our Lord's entrance into Jerusalem. The thurifer approaches, and incense is blessed as usual. The thurifer bows and joins the candle bearers; all face the celebrant. The deacon seeks the celebrant's blessing, as at a Solemn Mass.[5] Preceded by the thurifer and candle bearers, he goes to the lectern and proclaims the Gospel.[6] If there is no deacon or concelebrant, the celebrant prepares incense and goes to the lectern to read the Gospel. A brief homily may follow on the significance of Christ's entrance into Jerusalem.

139. Preparations are now made for the procession. The thurifer approaches; incense is blessed as usual; the thurifer bows and goes to a position to lead the procession with the cross bearer and candle bearers. The deacon or M.C. hands the celebrant his palm. The deacon or a concelebrant or, lacking either, the celebrant himself sings or says, "Let us go forth in peace, praising Jesus our Messiah . . .", or similar words, and the procession begins. Moving at a dignified pace, the procession follows this order: thurifer, cross bearer, candle bearers, choir and/or cantors, clergy in choir dress, deacon or lector carrying the Book of the Gospels, concelebrants, celebrant (with a second deacon) and the faithful carrying their palms.[7] All in the procession carry palms, unless they have to carry another object. Ushers should supervise the procession and maintain due order.

140. During the procession either the antiphon "The children of Jerusalem . . ." with verses of Psalm 23 or 46 or a similar

---

[5] See CMRR, nos. 384–87. If there is no deacon and a concelebrant reads the Gospel, he does not seek the blessing, unless the celebrant is a bishop; cf. CB, no. 173.

[6] See CMRR, nos. 388–89.

[7] In some places, children carry larger branches in the procession. They should be trained well and supervised by an adult.

hymn in honor of Christ the King is sung;[8] then a hymn such as "All Glory, Laud and Honor" is sung. If the celebrant wears a cope, two deacons, the deacon and M.C., or two servers may hold it back during the procession. It is assumed that this procession takes a long route, outside or even, if necessary, inside the church. Therefore the antiphon "The children of Jerusalem . . ." with the entrance versicle or an entrance hymn is only sung once the procession actually enters the church or begins to move down the aisle towards the sanctuary. The faithful go to their places at this stage, ushers guiding them if necessary.

141.   On arriving at the sanctuary, the servers go to their usual places. The deacon puts the Book of the Gospels on the altar and waits there. The celebrant comes before the altar; he hands his palm to the M.C. or a server (who takes it to the credence table) and then genuflects or bows. He goes to the altar, and (with the deacon[s]) he kisses it. The altar is incensed as usual.[9] More incense may be put in the thurible by a server just before the incensation of the altar. Then the celebrant goes to the chair. If the cope has been worn it is now removed and replaced by the chasuble. Attended by the book bearer, the celebrant sings or says "Let us pray" and the Opening Prayer of the Mass, which concludes the procession. The deacon, M.C. or a server assists the celebrant.[10] A server collects the palms of those who assist in the sanctuary and takes them to the credence table, where they are put on a salver or tray.

---

[8] Cf. CLE, no. 32.

[9] If the celebrant wears a cope, the deacon(s), deacon and M.C., concelebrants or the M.C. alone should hold it back to free his arms during the incensation, as is customary at Solemn Vespers, see CMRR, no. 734.

[10] A server should take the cope back to the sacristy.

142. The Liturgy of the Word follows. If the Reading of the Passion takes place at the ambo, and three books of the Passion
reading are to be used, at the end of the second reading,
the lector gives the Lectionary to a server, who takes it to
the credence table.

The Reading of the Passion

143. The Passion takes the place of the Gospel, but it is proclaimed without candles or incense. If they are not already
in place, three bare lecterns are set up (with microphones, if
necessary) at the center of the sanctuary or some other suitable place. All stand for the acclamation before the Gospel.
The vested deacons or lectors come from their places in
the sanctuary, each carrying a book of the Passion. Only
the deacons go to the celebrant at the chair and seek his
blessing. They bow for his blessing as usual and then go
directly to the lecterns or to the ambo. The narrator stands
at the central lectern (or ambo), Christus on his right, the
crowd on his left. "The Lord be with you" and the signing
of the book is omitted.[11] When possible, the Passion should
be sung, with the narrator and Christus and with the choir
taking the part of the crowd.[12] If there is no deacon and
the celebrant reads the Passion, he should take the part of
Christ.

144. All stand during the Passion.[13] After the verse recounting the
death of Our Lord, all kneel in silent prayer for a few moments. Those reading the Passion kneel facing the lecterns
or ambo. At the end of the reading, "(This is) the Gospel

---

[11] Cf. CB, no. 273.

[12] Some good vernacular versions of the classical settings of the Passion are
now available.

[13] The elderly and mothers with small children should be advised to sit, otherwise standing for the Passion should be maintained.

of the Lord" is sung or said, but the book is not kissed.[14] Those who read the Passion take their books, come before the altar, bow to it and return to their places. The lecterns are removed by servers. A homily follows, but pastoral experience indicates that this should be short, to allow the proclaimed Passion to speak for itself. As at Good Friday, the faithful may be invited to spend a short time in meditation after the homily.

The Bishop Presides on Palm Sunday

145.   The bishop wears a red cope or chasuble and the ornate miter, and he carries the crozier. After he has blessed the palms, he receives his palm from the deacon or a concelebrant. Then he may set aside his palm and distribute palms to the clergy and some of the faithful. He holds his palm during the reading of the Gospel. The Book of the Gospels may, and should, be brought to him to be kissed immediately after the Gospel has been read by the deacon or a concelebrant. Either the bishop or the deacon sings or says, "Let us go forth in peace, praising Jesus our Messiah . . .", or similar words at the beginning of the procession. Because the bishop carries a palm during the procession, the crozier bearer walks directly in front of him, carrying the crozier within the vimpa. The book bearer and miter bearer follow him, preceding the faithful in the procession. If the cope has been worn, it is replaced by the chasuble after the incensation of the altar, just before the Opening Prayer of the Mass.[15] If other deacons proclaim the Passion, they may

---

[14] Cf. CB, no. 273, clarifying what is not clear in the Lectionary or some editions of the Passion.

[15] CB, no. 271, also offers the option of removing the cope on arriving at the altar, before reverencing and incensing the altar, but this would impede the continuity of the ceremonial movement.

carry the books of the Passion in the procession.[16] Before
the Reading of the Passion, the bishop blesses the deacons
and/or any concelebrant who will take a part in it.

Second Form: Solemn Entrance

146. The solemn entrance takes place within the church and
should only be chosen when it is not possible to have a procession. The immediate preparations are made as above,
however the lectern for the Gospel is set up at the place
within the church where the Solemn Entrance will begin.
Before the ceremony, the ushers or servers distribute palms
to the faithful, either as they enter the church or once they
have gone to their seats.

147. The celebrant and servers, and some representatives of the
faithful carrying palms,[17] go in procession to a suitable place,
usually the narthex, a porch or an area just inside the main
door, or even an area directly outside the main door. If possible this procession should come from the sacristy without going through the church. Just as the procession arrives at this place the antiphon "Hosanna to the Son of
David . . ." or a suitable hymn is sung. Ushers and servers
assist the faithful, who should also be encouraged to turn to
face the place where the rite will be celebrated. The blessing
of palms, the Gospel and preparations for the procession follow exactly as set out above. In the procession through the
church, the representatives of the faithful follow the celebrant, carrying their palms. They go to their places when
the celebrant enters the sanctuary.

---

[16] Cf. CB, no. 270, which presupposes they are already vested in albs and red
stoles.
[17] Children carrying larger branches would be appropriate representatives of
the faithful.

148. However, if the procession goes directly to the altar from the place where the palms were blessed, the antiphon or the hymn may well replace the entrance antiphon or entrance hymn. Another possibility would be for the solemn entrance to take the form of a longer procession around the interior of the church, with the appropriate antiphon, etc., and for the antiphon and responsory or entrance hymn to begin only when the procession begins to move down the main aisle towards the altar.[18] Once the celebrant and servers have arrived at the sanctuary, the Mass begins, as described above. The readings and the Passion follow, as described above.

Third Form: Simple Entrance

149. This simpler rite may be used at other Masses during the day. In fact it is only an entrance procession during which the antiphon "Six days . . ." and Psalm 23:9–10 are sung.[19] To make this action more significant, palms should be distributed to the faithful before Mass, the cross decorated with palms should be carried in the procession, and incense should be used.

150. At all the simpler Masses on this day, it seems preferable for the Reading of the Passion to be planned with a lector as the narrator, the celebrant as Christus, and the congregation taking the place of other characters and the crowd.[20] Whatever form the rites take, it is customary for the faithful to take blessed palms home, to serve as a reminder of the victory of Christ celebrated in the procession.[21] At home,

---

[18] As for the Presentation of the Lord, where the solemn procession outdoors would take place under normal circumstances, this alternative would be a good way of celebrating the rite during inclement weather.

[19] Or some other hymn, such as "All Glory, Laud and Honor", may be sung.

[20] This involves the people directly as "assistants at the Passion". Everyone must have a clearly marked text for participation.

[21] Cf. CLE, no. 29.

the blessed palms may be set up behind a crucifix or other image. After the Masses and ceremonies on Passion Sunday, remaining palms that will provide ashes for the next Ash Wednesday should be stored in the sacristy. During the first days of Holy Week, blessed palms may be left on a table inside the church to be taken to those who were unable to take part in the ceremonies.[22] Information about the time of the ceremonies of the Sacred Triduum and Easter together with times when priests will be available for the Sacrament of Penance must be provided at all Masses on Palm Sunday.

Holy Week

151. From Monday to Thursday inclusive, the days of Holy Week take precedence over all other celebrations. Therefore, feasts and memorials of saints that happen to fall in Holy Week are not observed, nor is it fitting that the sacraments of Baptism and Confirmation be celebrated until the Easter Vigil.[23] The first four days of Holy Week should offer opportunities for celebrations of the First and Second Rites of Reconciliation, the Way of the Cross and other devotions and processions that are part of the local culture or customary among groups within the community.[24] On the evening of the Wednesday, a form of Tenebræ may be celebrated.[25]

152. In close collaboration with the M.C., sacristans, servers, music director, catechists, etc., the pastor and his assistants

---

[22] Clergy and those authorized to distribute the Eucharist to the sick or aged at home, in hospitals or rest homes should also bring them a blessed palm.

[23] Cf. CLE, no. 27.

[24] Holy Week is a time when pastors should respect local devotional customs and the practices of ethnic groups in the parish community.

[25] See appendix 7, "Tenebræ".

should ensure that precise preparations are made for the ceremonial and music of Holy Thursday, Good Friday and the Easter Vigil. *Nothing* must be left to chance. Booklets should be available for the faithful to ensure their full and active participation in the noble rites of the Sacred Triduum. Because it is somewhat complex and may not necessarily take place during the Triduum, the Mass of the Chrism is described in the following chapter.

The Word of God the Father,
the Son who is coeternal with Him,
whose throne is heaven, whose footstool is the earth,
today has humbled himself by riding into Bethany on
a donkey.
So the children of Israel praise him,
bearing green branches and crying:
"Hosanna in the highest! Blessed is he who comes,
the King of Israel!"

— from the Byzantine Vespers,
Stichera for Palm Sunday

6.

Mass of the Chrism

153. Jesus is "the Christ", the Messiah, the Anointed One. He is our eternal High Priest, who incorporates us into his living Body, the Church, giving us a share in his Priesthood in different ways. In the sacramental liturgy of the bishop of the particular Church, we are raised into the saving effects of the Paschal Mystery through the effective sign of anointing with blessed Oil. We are prepared for the journey of faith with the Oil of Catechumens; we are permanently sealed by the Holy Spirit with the fragrant Chrism of prophets, priests and kings; we are strengthened in this life and sent forth into eternity with the healing and pardon of the Oil of the Sick.

154. On the morning of Holy Thursday, the Mass of the Chrism should be solemnly celebrated in the cathedral by the Ordinary himself.[1] However, for pastoral reasons it may be celebrated in another suitable church. It can be transferred to a day earlier in Holy Week, for a good reason, for example, to enable the clergy of the diocese to gather and concelebrate the Eucharistic Sacrifice at a time when they are free from parish commitments.[2] The priests gather around their bishop to express the unity of the priesthood and Christ's one Sacrifice. They assist their bishop "as witnesses and

---

[1] In case of necessity, he may delegate another bishop to consecrate Chrism and bless the Oils.

[2] It may even be celebrated on the morning or evening of Monday, Tuesday or Wednesday in Holy Week, cf. MR, *Mass of the Chrism*, no. 3.

cooperators in the consecration of Chrism", thereby affirming how they share in his sacred office of building up, sanctifying and governing the Church.[3] Therefore, priests representing all the regions or deaneries in the diocese should concelebrate this Mass. Likewise, lay representatives from all parts of the diocese should take part in the Mass to witness the renewal of priestly commitment and pray for the clergy. Catholic youth and schoolchildren should also be able to take part in this noble Mass, which has such rich sacramental and vocational meanings, especially for those preparing for Confirmation.

155. There are two ways of incorporating the consecration of Chrism and the blessing of the Oil of Catechumens and the Oil of the Sick into the Mass: (1) by blessing the Oil of the Sick during the Eucharistic Prayer and then blessing the Oil of Catechumens and consecrating the Chrism after the Prayer after Communion; (2) by blessing the Oils and consecrating the Chrism after the homily and Renewal of Commitment to Priestly Service.[4] The former is the traditional practice. However, because it is a simpler procedure, the latter may be chosen for pastoral reasons.[5]

156. All the usual preparations are made for a Solemn Pontifical Mass celebrated by the Ordinary. If three or more deacons are not available to bear the Oils, concelebrants may appropriately take their place. However, while a deacon or priest is specified to bear the Oil of Chrism, other ministers may bear the Oil of Catechumens, the Oil of the Sick

---

[3] Cf. CB, no. 274.

[4] The second option is the current practice at the papal liturgy in Rome and has become widespread. Nevertheless, the traditional practice clearly distinguishes the Oil used to anoint the sick and dying from the Oil of Catechumens and Chrism for initiating Christians.

[5] Cf. MR, *Mass of the Chrism*, no. 5.

and the vessel of balsam or perfume.[6] The Oils should be contained in three truly noble vessels, made of any suitable material and clearly marked as *Chrism* (Ch.), *Oil of Catechumens* (Cat.) and *Oil of the Sick* (Inf.).[7] If the vessels are large and heavy, they should have handles attached so that two persons can carry them, one on each side. A smaller noble vessel of balsam or perfume and a long metal spoon or similar implement is required for mingling the aromatic substance with Chrism. But if the bishop does not wish to mix the Chrism during the Mass, the sacristan must carefully attend to this beforehand.[8] If the crosses are already veiled, the altar crucifix and/or processional crucifix may be veiled in white for this celebration, as is the custom at the evening Mass of the Lord's Supper.

Immediate Preparations

157. *Altar*: seven candles lit, if the Ordinary is the celebrant, otherwise six or four (white antependium).

158. *Ambo*: (white antependium); Lectionary, marked.

---

[6] For these distinctions, see CB, no. 282. Lacking deacons, it would seem preferable to designate seminarians in the clerical state or instituted acolytes to be the "ministers" who bear Oils. They should wear albs.

[7] The custom is retained in some places of also having a distinctively colored silk veil for each vessel: white or gold for Chrism, green for the Oil of Catechumens, violet for the Oil of the Sick. The deacons or ministers bearing the Oils may wear this veil like a vimpa, enveloping their hands and covering the top of the vessel.

[8] (a) A rich balsam or strong essence of perfume should be chosen and carefully blended, so that even the smallest amount of Chrism is fragrant. (b) The balsam or perfume may best be mixed into the oil before Mass, then only a symbolic amount would be added by the bishop during the rite. The sacristan must ensure that the Chrism is properly blended before the Oils are bottled and distributed to the clergy.

159. *Table of the Oils*: a dignified and secure table, covered with a fine cloth or noble fabric, set at one side of the sanctuary.

160. *Credence table*: the usual requirements for pontifical Mass. The Missal containing the propers and the prayers for the blessing of Oils may be here or near the cathedra.

161. *Table of gifts*: not used for this Mass, or it is set up in the chapel where the vessels of oil have been prepared.

162. *Sacristy or vesting room*: white eucharistic vestments for the bishop, deacons and concelebrants,[9] white dalmatics for any other deacons who bear the oils, the three large vessels filled with oil, more if necessary, each clearly marked (a vessel for balsam or perfume and a spoon, if required during the Mass), bread, wine and water for the procession of gifts. Alternatively, these vessels of oil and eucharistic gifts may be prepared in a chapel.

163. The liturgy follows the form of a solemn concelebrated stational or pontifical Mass as described in *Ceremonies of the Modern Roman Rite*, nos. 473–507. The three (or more) deacons who will later bear the oils precede the concelebrants in the entrance procession.[10]

164. The bishop may preach from the cathedra, seated or standing, wearing the miter and, if he so wishes, holding the crozier. At the conclusion of the homily he remains seated, still wearing the miter. If he has not been holding it during the homily, he receives the crozier. The book bearer attends him with the Missal. All priests present stand for the

---

[9] This concelebration underlines the need to have complete matching sets of eucharistic vestments for all the clergy of the diocese.

[10] That is, unless they are the deacon(s) of the Mass and the bishop's two assistant deacons.

Renewal of Commitment to Priestly Service, which takes the form of three questions with the response "I am". If possible, they should come forward and stand before the bishop.[11] After the third question, the bishop stands and gives up the crozier and miter. As indicated in the Missal, he invites the people to pray for their priests and for himself. The Creed is omitted.[12]

165. The bishop sits and receives the miter. The deacons, ministers or concelebrants who will bear the Oils go to the sacristy, vesting room or chapel where the vessels of oil and eucharistic gifts have been prepared. Servers or laity who will present the eucharistic gifts meet them there, where they are assisted by an M.C., sacristan or server. Meanwhile, directed by the M.C., servers place the table of the Oils at the center of the sanctuary.[13] Quiet music may accompany these preparations. Then the deacons and ministers bring the vessels of oil in procession, followed by servers or members of the faithful carrying the eucharistic gifts of bread, wine and water. The procession should not take the shortest route but rather be seen to pass through the cathedral. During the procession the choir leads the singing of "O Redemptor" or another suitable hymn. The hymn should cease once the bearers of the vessels of oil arrive before the altar and have taken positions facing the cathedra. Because

---

[11] Cf. CB, no. 280. In a large diocese, at least consultors, members of the senate of priests and/or priests representing deaneries, regions or particular forms of priestly ministry may come forward and stand before the bishop for the Renewal of Commitment to Priestly Service.

[12] But the General Intercessions are not omitted, cf. MR, *Mass of the Chrism*, no. 10.

[13] (a) The Oils and Chrism are never blessed and consecrated *on* the altar. (b) However, if the table would impede ceremonies, it may remain at the side and the deacons would take the vessels of oil there after presenting them to the bishop. Then the table could be brought forward during Communion.

they bear the oil, they make no reverence to the altar or the bishop.

166.   The bishop receives the vessels of oil and the gifts either at the cathedra or at some other suitable place, such as in front of or behind the table of the Oils, if this is already in place at the center of the sanctuary. Once the processional hymn has finished, the deacon, minister or concelebrant bearing each vessel of oil comes to the bishop and sings or says "The oil for the holy Chrism", or "The oil of the sick" or "The oil of catechumens", in that order and depending on what vessel he carries. He may appropriately raise the vessel somewhat as he presents it. The bishop takes each vessel of oil, if this is convenient, and hands it to an assistant deacon, concelebrant or server, who takes it to the table of the Oils. If the vessel is large and heavy, the bishop simply lays his hand on it and two of the bearers take it to the table of the Oils. It may be found more convenient for the bearers to receive the vessels of oil back from the bishop and then take them to the table of the Oils, whether this is set up at the center or at the side of the sanctuary.

167.   Servers or laity now bring the eucharistic gifts to the bishop. He hands them to deacons and/or servers, who take the patens and/or ciboria to the altar and the wine and water to the credence table. Servers also bring the corporal, chalice(s) and the Missal and its stand and arrange them on the altar as usual. If, for pastoral reasons, the blessing of Oils and consecration of Chrism follows immediately, the rite follows option (2), nos. 172–73 below. Otherwise the Mass continues as usual, and the bishop goes to the altar for the Preparation of the Gifts.

(1) Blessing the Oils and Consecrating Chrism
in the Course of the Liturgy of the Eucharist

168. The Preface of the Priesthood is used. During the Eucharistic Prayer, after the Consecration, at the naming of the martyrs in Eucharistic Prayer 1 or the memento of the dead in the other Eucharistic Prayers, the deacon, minister or concelebrant who bears the oil to be blessed for the sick brings the vessel of oil to the altar. He stands at the center, facing the bishop on the other side of the altar. The book bearer, carrying the Missal, may attend the bishop, unless, as may be more convenient, the Missal remains on the altar. The deacon or M.C. turns to the prayer for the blessing in the proper of the Mass of the Chrism.[14] The Oil of the Sick is now blessed, that is, just before the bishop says "through Christ our Lord you give us all these gifts", in Eucharistic Prayer 1, or just before he sings the doxology in the other Eucharistic Prayers. During the prayer of blessing, the bearer may raise the vessel somewhat to accentuate the act of blessing. At the conclusion of the prayer, he reverently takes the Oil of the Sick to the table of the Oils. The Eucharistic Prayer concludes as usual.

169. After the Prayer after Communion, the bishop sits and receives the miter. The deacon(s), ministers and/or concelebrants bring the vessels of oil for the Oil of Catechumens and the Chrism (and the smaller vessel of balsam or perfume, if this has not already been mingled in the Chrism) and place them on the table of the Oils set up at the center of the sanctuary—unless they have already been in place

---

[14] If Mass is celebrated "facing the altar", the book bearer brings the Missal, and the bishop turns to face the people for the blessing of the Oil of the Sick, but preferably in such a way as not to turn his back on the Holy Eucharist.

there since the procession of the gifts. Taking his crozier, flanked by the assistant deacons, the bishop comes from the cathedra and stands facing the people, directly behind the table. The M.C. arranges the concelebrants around the bishop in a semi-circle.[15] The deacons and servers attending the bishop stand directly behind him. He gives the crozier and the miter to an assistant deacon, who gives the miter and crozier to their respective bearers. The book bearer approaches with the Missal opened at the appropriate page, and the bishop proceeds to bless the Oil of Catechumens. He extends his hands and says the prayer, "Lord God, Protector of all . . .", making the sign of the cross over the Oil at "bless this oil". The deacon or M.C. customarily removes the cover from the vessel of oil during the blessing.

170. If the balsam or perfume has not been mixed with the Chrism, the bishop receives the miter. The deacon or M.C. uncovers the vessel of oil for the Chrism, and the bishop pours the aromatic substance into the oil, carefully mixing it with a large spoon or another convenient instrument.[16] Then the miter is removed.

171. With his hands joined, the bishop sings or says the invitation "Let us pray that God. . . ." Then he may incline forward slightly and breathe over the Chrism, customarily in the form of a cross. He extends his hands and sings or says one of the two consecratory prayers provided in the Pontifical, making the sign of the cross at the words indicated in the text. All concelebrants hold their right hands outstretched towards the Chrism from "And so Father . . ."

---

[15] When there are many concelebrants, this may not be feasible. But consultors, members of the senate or priests, or representatives of the deaneries or regions of the diocese, could form this semi-circle around the bishop.

[16] According to CB, no. 289, he should be seated while mixing Chrism, but this does not seem to be convenient or necessary.

until the end of the prayer, but they say nothing. After the Chrism has been consecrated, supervised by the M.C., the concelebrants return to their places. The bishop receives the miter and crozier and returns to the cathedra. The final blessing and procession follow, as described below in nos. 174–76.

(2) Blessing the Oils and Consecrating Chrism after the Liturgy of the Word

172. Having received the vessels of oil and the gifts at the cathedra, the bishop takes his crozier and goes to stand behind the table of the Oils. However, when the Oils are blessed after the Liturgy of the Word, it would be simpler for him to receive the vessels of oil and the eucharistic gifts standing in front of the table of the Oils, and then to go and stand behind it for the rite of blessing.[17] The concelebrants, deacons and servers gather around him as described above. He gives the crozier and miter to a server, and, attended by the book bearer carrying the Missal, he blesses the Oil of the Sick as described above in no. 168. He blesses the Oil of Catechumens as described above in no. 169. Finally, he consecrates the Chrism as described above in nos. 170–71.

173. After the consecration of the Chrism, the concelebrants return to their places. The bishop takes his miter and crozier and returns to the cathedra, where he waits while the preparation of the altar is completed. If the altar has already been prepared, he goes directly to the altar for the Preparation of the Gifts. Meanwhile, the bearers of the Oils may take up the vessels of blessed Oils while servers move the table

---

[17] If the table is not deep, the bishop may stand behind it when receiving the oils.

to the side of the sanctuary. The bearers then place the Oils back on the table. Mass continues as usual. The Preface of the Priesthood is used. The final blessing and procession are described in the paragraphs that follow.

(1) and (2): The Procession of the Blessed Oils and Holy Chrism

174. At the cathedra, the bishop gives the final blessing, but the deacon does not sing the dismissal at this stage. The bishop then hands the crozier to an assistant deacon and sits. The thurifer approaches and bows to the bishop, who prepares and blesses an ample amount of incense for the procession. The thurifer bows and goes to the center of the sanctuary to join the cross bearer and candle bearers to lead the procession. Meanwhile, the deacons, ministers or concelebrants who bear the Oils go to the table, take up the Oils and move to a position so that they will come immediately after the thurifer, cross bearer and candle bearers in the procession. The bishop stands and takes the crozier. The deacon sings the dismissal. The bishop and deacons go to the altar and kiss it. The customary reverences are made, and the procession begins.

175. As the blessed Oils are solemnly borne in procession, the hymn "O Redemptor" or some other appropriate hymn is sung. On arrival in the sacristy, the Oils are set down in a suitable place. The bishop may instruct the priests present about the reverent use and safe custody of the blessed Oils, preferably before the clergy remove their vestments.

176. The Oils are carefully transferred to clearly labeled bottles as soon as possible, so that clergy who assisted at the rite can take them back to their parishes and replace the Oils in the repository and in the smaller oil stocks.[18] The cathedral sacristans should supervise seminarians or religious who appropriately carry out the duty of preparing bottles of the Oils for the clergy. In many places it is customary to celebrate the fraternity of the presbyterium with a dinner or reception at which the bishop presides.

The Reception of the Holy Oils
Blessed at the Chrism Mass

177. On Holy Thursday, the blessed Oils can be brought to the parish before the Mass of the Lord's Supper or at some other suitable time. The reception of the blessed Oils has pastoral value because it can be the occasion for catechesis on the use and the effects of the Chrism and blessed Oils.[19] A liturgical celebration for receiving the blessed Oils and placing them in their repository can be arranged more conveniently if the Mass takes place before Holy Thursday. In the United States the reception of the Oils may take place at the Mass of the Lord's Supper on Holy Thursday or on another suitable day if the Mass of the Chrism has been celebrated earlier in Holy Week.

178. Members of the community carry the Oils, in noble vessels, in the procession of the gifts, before the bread and wine. The celebrant receives them and places them either on a suitably prepared table in the sanctuary or directly in the repository, if it is nearby. A formula may be used as each of the Oils is presented, followed by a people's response, see

---

[18] The old Oils are either burned or consumed in lamps, see CMRR, no. 154. While the validity of the Oils remains (cf. CIC, Canon 847 §2), the old Oils should not normally be used for Christian Initiation at Easter.

[19] Cf. CLE, no. 36.

appendix 6. This practice is appropriate in the context of a parish program for the Rite of Christian Initiation of Adults. The catechumens should be involved in the celebration, but it seems preferable that they should not carry the Oils in the procession of gifts as their sacramental incorporation into the Church is not yet complete.

179. If the Oils are received during the Mass of the Lord's Supper and have been placed on a table in the sanctuary, the celebrant, deacon or a concelebrant takes them to the repository, without ceremony, after the procession to the "altar of repose". However, if the Oils are received at some other Mass, it would seem appropriate that they be taken in procession to the repository at the end of Mass. A procedure similar to the Chrism Mass may well be followed. If incense is used, the celebrant prepares and blesses it after the Prayer after Communion. The thurifer goes to the center of the sanctuary to join the cross bearer and candle bearers to lead the procession. Meanwhile, deacons, concelebrants or members of the faithful who carry the Oils go to the table, take up the Oils and move to a position so that they will come immediately after the thurifer, cross bearer and candle bearers in the procession.[20] The deacon or celebrant sings the dismissal, and the procession goes first to the repository and from there to the sacristy.

---

[20] However, the celebrant or another priest should carry the Chrism.

Be sure, however, not to regard the Chrism as a mere ointment. Just as after the invocation of the Holy Spirit the Bread of the Eucharist is no longer just bread but the Body of Christ, so when the Holy Spirit has been invoked on the sacred Chrism it is no longer merely an ordinary ointment. It is Christ's gift which instills his divinity into us through the presence of the Holy Spirit. With a symbolic meaning it is applied to your forehead and sense organs. Just as the body is anointed with a visible ointment, so the soul is sanctified by the hidden Holy Spirit.

— Instructions to the Newly Baptized at Jerusalem
Mystagogic Catechesis, 3.3

7.

Holy Thursday

180. At the summit of the Church year, the three great days of the Easter Triduum encompass the Paschal Mystery and draw us into the Passion, death and Resurrection of Jesus our Savior. With his disciples, we enter the upper room to celebrate the Passover. We accompany him to watch at his agony in Gethsemane, and then we follow him through the halls of judgment to his bitter Passion. We take his way of sorrow that leads to Calvary and death on a cross. Then we assist at his burial in the rock tomb. We wait in solemn vigil until he rises again, in our human flesh, glorious and immortal. So we look in hope to our compassionate High Priest returning to the Father and taking us to glory with him in his Mystical Body, the Church.

The Easter Triduum

181. In the evening of Holy Thursday the Triduum begins. The first two days of the Triduum, Good Friday and Holy Saturday, make up the Easter fast, when the Church follows the ancient tradition of fasting because "the Bridegroom has been taken away" (cf. Mark 2:19–20). The fast is obligatory on Good Friday, but recommended on Holy Saturday.[1] The ceremonies of the Triduum should be planned carefully. A sufficient number of servers and other assistants should be

---

[1] Cf. CLE, no. 39.

rostered and trained thoroughly so that they know their roles in the ceremonies. At the same time, pastors must ensure that the meaning of each part of the celebration is explained to the faithful for active and fruitful participation.[2]

182. Music is essential to the worthy celebration of the "Easter ceremonies". Even in the smallest church, with limited resources, every effort should be made to provide some appropriate liturgical music for the rites of the Triduum. In major churches with a choir and musicians, the music should draw on the rich heritage of the Church, both ancient and modern, while ensuring that this does not impede the active participation of the faithful.[3]

183. In some places the ceremonies cannot be carried out well, due to such factors as small congregations, lack of clergy, servers, musicians, etc. Then the smaller community should be invited to a nearby church where the ceremonies can be carried out with due solemnity. This is particularly relevant when one priest has responsibility for several churches. Likewise, small lay, clerical or religious communities should come to a neighboring major church for the ceremonies, rather than attempt to celebrate them for themselves.[4] The private celebration of the ceremonies, or extra celebrations for religious movements and spiritual groups, can also have a divisive effect when provision has been made for parish celebrations. Seminarians should participate in the Easter ceremonies as part of their formation, and especially when the bishop presides.[5] It is customary in some dioceses for

---

[2] Cf. CLE, no. 41.

[3] Cf. CLE, no. 42; a matter of balance, for "participation" is also a matter of listening and reflecting.

[4] Cf. CLE, no. 43.

[5] Ibid.

seminarians to act as servers at the cathedral during the Triduum.

Evening Mass of the Lord's Supper

184. In the evening of Holy Thursday, we celebrate the three gifts Jesus Christ imparted to his beloved Bride the Church: the Priesthood, the Eucharist and a Love that is stronger than death. In her liturgical rites, holy Church enters the upper room for the "Cena Domini". He, the Lord and Master of all, kneels humbly to wash the feet of the men he has called to serve. At table with his closest disciples, the Lord brings together all the sacrifices of the Old Law as he takes bread and wine and makes himself the one Sacrifice of a new dispensation, the Sacrifice of his Church. Then together they go forth into the night, to the Mount of Olives, to the Garden of Gethsemane, and the drama of his Passion begins.

185. As the sacred re-enactment of these moments, the evening Mass of the Lord's Supper is celebrated at a convenient hour, that is, at a time when the faithful can participate. The Mass usually includes the Washing of the Feet, and it always ends with the Solemn Transfer of the Holy Eucharist to the place of reposition. Taking into account a pastoral need, the diocesan bishop may permit another Mass, without the ceremonies, to be celebrated in churches or public or semi-public oratories, and for serious reasons such a Mass could even be celebrated in the morning. But this provision is exclusively for those unable to be at the evening Mass.[6] Priests who concelebrated at the Mass of the Chrism in the morning, or who celebrated another permitted Mass, may

---

[6] Cf. MR, *Evening Mass of the Lord's Supper*, no. 3, adding that such a provision is not to be made for private persons or in a way that would prejudice the principal evening Mass.

concelebrate again at the evening Mass. On this day, outside the celebration of the Mass of the Lord's Supper, or other permitted Masses, the Eucharist is only given to the sick or as Viaticum. Vespers is recited by those who do not participate in the Mass of the Lord's Supper.

186. The *Place of Reposition* should be as beautiful as possible, to invite the faithful to "watch with the Lord". If the church has a Blessed Sacrament chapel, it is appropriate for this to become the place of reposition.[7] However, it may seem preferable to prepare some other chapel or area that is not normally used for eucharistic reservation, especially if this is some distance from the sanctuary, to allow for a significant procession. For the same reason, the place of reposition should not be set up in the sanctuary because the Eucharistic Procession itself represents a distinct movement from one place, the "Cena Domini", to another place, the Garden of Gethsemane.[8] Therefore a chapel within or next to the church or a dignified room adjacent to the church should be carefully prepared as the place of reposition. The "altar of repose" does not necessarily have to be a real altar, but it is customary to make it resemble an altar.

187. A tabernacle or a similar secure repository (formerly known as the "urn") is used for the eucharistic reposition.[9] It is not veiled. Candles, at least four or six, preferably more,

---

[7] Cf. CLE, no. 49.

[8] Liturgical minimalism prevails if "the place of reposition" means merely some extra candles and flowers near the tabernacle in the sanctuary. Then the procession would go around the church only to return to where it began. This could only be tolerated in a small church where there was no other suitable place for reposition.

[9] According to CLE, no. 55, a ciborium (pyx) may be used, apparently when a closed tabernacle is not available, and obviously with provision for the faithful to keep watch in order to avoid profanation. But exposition in a monstrance is forbidden at the place of reposition.

together with lamps and flowers are arranged on and around the "altar of repose", according to resources and local custom. The walls around the place of reposition may be draped with noble hangings and a fine carpet may be placed on the pavement and steps.[10] If the faithful carry candles in the procession, candelabra, a pricket stand or a sandbox should be prepared where they can later leave their candles. If there is a crucifix, sacred image or a reredos with images directly behind the chapel altar, it should be removed or veiled, preferably in white, so that the Holy Eucharist predominates. Suitable seating with kneeling benches should be prepared for the faithful who will keep watch with the Lord.[11]

188. The Blessed Sacrament is privately removed from the tabernacle in the church before the Mass begins and taken to a "place of reservation", that is, a tabernacle or safe in the sacristy or in an oratory or chapel apart from the church. The Hosts reserved here will provide an extra supply for Holy Communion on Good Friday. A lamp should burn in this place, but adoration is not maintained here.

189. If the Washing of the Feet is to be part of the Mass, men from among the faithful, twelve or fewer, are chosen.[12] They should be notified well before Holy Thursday and not called

---

[10] The place of reposition should not resemble a tomb, because the chapel of repose does not represent the Lord's burial. We do not follow the custom of three days of reservation in an "Easter sepulcher", which was the pre-Reformation practice in England.

[11] A roster of those who will adore should be planned beforehand, especially to ensure an adequate number to watch in the late hours, or, where customary, if simple adoration continues beyond the end of solemn adoration at midnight. Where the excellent practice of perpetual adoration is established, this will be the duty of the organizing committee for this apostolate.

[12] The rubric stipulates "men" (*viri*), for a re-enactment of the washing of the feet of the apostles; cf. MR, *Mass of the Lord's Supper, Washing of Feet*, no. 11; CB, no. 301; CLE, no. 51. No number is specified, but the prevailing tradition is twelve.

up at the last moment. The procedure described below should be clearly explained to them, and they should be seated near the sanctuary so that they may be conveniently led to the place where their feet will be washed.[13]

190. Everything is prepared for a Solemn Mass, with deacon(s), concelebrants and M.C. and the full complement of servers: cross and candle bearers, thurifer(s), book bearer, two, four or six torch bearers. Two thuribles may, and should, be used for the Transfer of the Holy Eucharist.[14] Members of the faithful, carrying hand candles, may, and should, take part in the procession or Transfer of the Holy Eucharist, even when the whole congregation cannot take part.

191. Where the Mass takes a simpler form, without a deacon, an M.C. should direct the ceremonies, adapting what is described below. If possible, there should be at least a thurifer, cross and candle bearers with a book bearer. These servers assist the celebrant at the Washing of the Feet. Incense should be used during this Mass,[15] and must be used during the Transfer of the Holy Eucharist. Members of the faithful, carrying hand candles, would also enrich a simpler form of this procession.

Immediate Preparations

192. *Altar*: six or four candles, lit (white antependium); the altar crucifix may be veiled in white.

---

[13] To substitute washing hands for feet misses the whole point of this action and surely has unfortunate connotations at this time, cf. Matthew 27:24.

[14] Cf. CB, 307, which restores and requires the former practice when the bishop presides, thus correcting MR, *Evening Mass of the Lord's Supper, Transfer of the Holy Eucharist*.

[15] Incense is obligatory when the bishop celebrates the Mass of the Lord's Supper; cf. CB, no. 300.

193. *Ambo*: (white antependium).

194. *Chair*: book of the chair or order of Holy Week.

195. *Credence table*: the usual requirements for Mass together with extra ciboria with an ample supply of bread to be consecrated for Communion on Good Friday; bells to be rung during the Gloria (wooden clapper if customary for use at the Consecration). Here or on another table: a large ewer of water, a basin and twelve towels on a tray for the washing of the feet, a linen gremial or amice, several tapers, hand candles for clergy and servers.

196. *Table of gifts*: bread, wine and water for the procession of gifts (ample supply of bread for Communion on Good Friday).

197. *Sanctuary*: two benches or twelve chairs for the washing of the feet; a white humeral veil draped over a stand or folded elsewhere.

198. *Tabernacle*: empty, open and without a veil (even if it will later become the place of reposition).

199. *Place of Reposition*: a corporal spread in front of the tabernacle, the key, but the candles and lamps remain unlit until during the time of Communion.

200. *Sacristy*: white vestments for celebrant, deacon(s), concelebrants; a second thurible may and should be prepared. If the processional crucifix is veiled, the veil should be white.

201. Solemn Mass is concelebrated as usual. During the Gloria, the church bells, and other bells, are rung and then remain silent until the Gloria at the Easter Vigil.[16] In the homily, the celebrant should develop the meanings of this sacred night of the "Cena Domini": the mystery of the Eucharist, the Priesthood and the Love of Jesus, the One who kneels to serve.[17] The hymns chosen should reflect these themes.

The Washing of the Feet

202. After the homily, the celebrant returns to the chair, and preparations are made for the Washing of the Feet. If they are not already in place, the benches or chairs are brought forward by servers. The twelve men whose feet are to be washed are led by a server or usher to the benches or chairs. They sit and customarily remove footwear and hosiery from the right foot. Meanwhile, assisted by the deacon, M.C. or a server, the celebrant removes his chasuble, which is draped over the chair. He may put on a linen gremial or amice as an apron, which a server brings to him from the credence table. When those whose feet are to be washed have taken their places, the first candle bearer brings the ewer, and the second candle bearer brings the basin and the towels from the credence table. A third server could accompany them, with the towels on a tray, which will be collected after they have been used. They meet the celebrant, deacon(s) and M.C. at the center of the sanctuary. The celebrant, deacon(s) and M.C. bow to the altar and, followed by the candle bearers with the ewer, etc., they go to the first of those whose feet

---

[16] "As will be noted below for the Easter Vigil, the bells may be pealed loudly, but briefly, before the Gloria is intoned, or they may be rung during the Gloria in a way that does not interfere with the singing, or, with due musical skill they may even be rung as part of the setting of the Gloria. At the very least, the candle bearers could briefly ring 'sanctus bells' at the credence table just before the Gloria."

[17] Cf. MR, *Evening Mass of the Lord's Supper*, no. 9, and see CCC, nos. 1120, 1544–45, 1548, 1562–68.

are to be washed. One or more of the six antiphons or a similar hymn or motet is now sung.

203.   The Washing of the Feet should be carried out at a steady, reverent pace, without haste. The celebrant kneels before each man.[18] The deacon kneels on his right and receives the ewer from the first candle bearer, who kneels on his right. The deacon gives the ewer to the celebrant, who pours water over the right foot into the basin, held by another deacon, or the M.C. or second candle bearer, who kneels on the celebrant's left. Then the celebrant hands the ewer back to the deacon on his right. The second candle bearer gives one of the twelve towels to the celebrant, and he carefully dries the foot. He hands the used towel back to the candle bearer, who may pass it back to a third server standing behind him. The celebrant and assistants then stand and go on to the next man, and this procedure is repeated until the feet of all twelve have been washed.[19] When there is no deacon, the first candle bearer assists the celebrant with the ewer, kneeling on his right; the M.C. with the basin and the second candle bearer with the towels assist him, kneeling on his left.

204.   Then the celebrant and his assistants return to the center of the sanctuary. They bow to the altar. The celebrant and deacon(s) go to the chair where the gremial is removed, and a server takes it back to the credence table. The celebrant sits, and servers bring a jug, bowl and towel from the credence table to wash his hands,[20] and then he stands and puts on his chasuble. Meanwhile, the candle bearers take

---

[18] He does not "walk" on his knees from person to person. It is a gracious custom for him to bow to each man before kneeling to wash his feet.

[19] During the rite, nothing is said to those whose feet are being washed.

[20] Cf. CB, no. 302, which logically also applies to priests.

the ewer, basin and towels used for the Washing of the Feet to the credence table or the sacristy. Servers or ushers escort those whose feet have been washed back to their places and remove the benches or chairs. The General Intercessions follow, but the Creed is omitted. If there is no Washing of the Feet, the General Intercessions follow the homily.[21]

205. The Mass continues as usual. The antiphon "Ubi caritas" or a similar hymn is sung during the procession of the gifts,[22] which should include gifts for the poor, perhaps linked to national or diocesan Lenten appeals for charity. When the First Eucharistic Prayer is chosen, there are variations at "In union with the whole Church . . .", "Father, accept this offering . . " and in the words just before the Consecration.[23] The bell is not rung at the elevations.[24] The torch bearers may remain in the sanctuary after the Eucharistic Prayer, as they will take part in the Transfer of the Holy Eucharist. Where it can be arranged conveniently, at the moment of Communion, it is appropriate that deacons, acolytes or extraordinary ministers take the Eucharist directly to the sick, so that they may be more closely united to the celebrating Church on this day.[25]

---

[21] Cf. MR, Holy Thursday, *Evening Mass of the Lord's Supper, Washing of the Feet*, no. 13.

[22] Cf. MR, *Evening Mass of the Lord's Supper, Liturgy of the Eucharist*, no. 14.

[23] Because of these variations, the First Eucharistic Prayer (Roman Canon) seems preferable on this night. The complete text of the prayer for Holy Thursday appears in the third edition of the *Missale Romanum*.

[24] In some places it is customary to use a wooden clapper.

[25] Cf. CLE, no. 53. After these ministers have received Communion themselves, they would place, or receive, an appropriate number of Hosts in a pyx and go at once to the sick.

The Transfer of the Holy Eucharist

206. During Communion preparations are quietly made for the solemn Transfer of the Holy Eucharist.[26] Servers or sacristans go to the place of reposition and light the candles and lamps. Hand candles are distributed to those in the sanctuary, the choir and laity who will take part in the Eucharistic Procession. The thurifer(s) and torch bearers genuflect and go to the sacristy to prepare charcoal for the thurible(s) and torches for the procession, that is, unless the torch bearers have remained in the sanctuary with their lighted torches. They return to the sanctuary immediately after the Prayer after Communion. If there is room, the torch bearers should form two parallel lines along the sanctuary, facing the altar, so that they are already in position to flank the celebrant as he comes from the altar carrying the Blessed Sacrament.

207. After Communion, the celebrant places the paten or ciborium on the altar and genuflects. He returns to the chair and sits. A server washes his hands. The deacon(s) or concelebrant(s) take the remaining Hosts from patens or ciboria and put them in one large ciborium (or large, covered paten), if this is possible. This ciborium is placed at the center of the corporal. If necessary, a priest, deacon, acolyte or another extraordinary minister immediately takes other ciboria containing Hosts to the "other place of reservation" in the sacristy or elsewhere.[27] Servers take the vessels that have been used for Communion to the credence table to be purified, now or after the procession. The Missal and its

---

[26] Note that the Transfer of the Eucharist is only carried out in churches where the Good Friday afternoon liturgy will be celebrated; cf. CLE, no. 54, citing the directives of the first reform of the ceremonies in 1956 and 1957.

[27] It seems preferable that only one ciborium be carried in procession to the "altar of repose".

stand are removed from the altar so that only the corporal and ciborium remain there.

208. A period of silent prayer or a psalm or hymn of praise follows. Then the celebrant stands, and, attended by the book bearer, he sings or says the Prayer after Communion. The blessing and dismissal are omitted. Servers now take tapers from the credence table and light the hand candles of the clergy and those members of the faithful who will take part in the procession.[28] Because they will lead the procession, the cross bearer and candle bearers go to the very front of the sanctuary or to the main aisle and wait there, facing the altar.

209. The celebrant, deacon(s) (or a concelebrant) and the M.C. come to the center of the sanctuary, or if there is no room here, they go to a central point immediately behind the altar. They genuflect. The thurifer approaches on the celebrant's right. Assisted by the deacon or a concelebrant or M.C., the celebrant prepares and blesses incense as usual (in both thuribles if a second thurifer also approaches from the right). Then the celebrant, deacon (or concelebrant) and M.C. kneel. All bow and (using the first thurible) the celebrant incenses the Eucharist with three double swings. They bow once more, and the celebrant hands the thurible to the deacon or M.C. The thurifer(s) may join the cross bearer and candle bearers at the center, but they take positions between them and the altar, because the cross bearer and candle bearers, not the thurifer, lead a Eucharistic Procession.

---

[28] When, as is usual in most places, all of the faithful cannot join in the procession, the representative group in the procession should include those whose feet were washed. This would strengthen the symbolism of the disciples leaving the upper room and going to Gethsemane.

210. The M.C. or a server places the humeral veil around the celebrant's shoulders. The celebrant secures the veil and stands. He goes to the altar, genuflects with the deacon (or concelebrant), from whom he receives the ciborium, enfolding it carefully under the veil. If no clergy assist, he takes the ciborium and arranges the veil himself. He returns to the center of the sanctuary, with the deacon or concelebrant. All turn to face the direction the procession will take and proceed on a signal from the M.C. The hymn "Pange, lingua" (up to the last two verses) or some other suitable eucharistic hymn is sung during the procession.[29] After the Prayer after Communion until the procession begins, quiet music may be played during the preparations for the procession, but the singing of the eucharistic hymn begins only when the procession commences.

211. The Transfer of the Holy Eucharist should move at a slow and reverent pace. The order of procession is as follows: the cross and candle bearers lead the procession, followed by a robed choir,[30] other servers without specific duties, clergy in choir dress, any deacons not assisting the celebrant, the concelebrants and finally the celebrant carrying the Holy Eucharist. Two, four or six torch bearers walk on each side of the celebrant.[31] He is flanked by two deacons or concelebrants, walking slightly behind him, and he is immediately preceded by the thurifer(s), as at the Eucharistic Procession of Corpus Christi.[32] All taking part in the procession carry

---

[29] If the procession is long, the hymn may be repeated or a second eucharistic hymn could be sung.

[30] A choir that is not robed follows the celebrant in the procession, carrying hand candles. According to circumstances, it may be preferable for the choir to remain in its place to lead the singing during the procession.

[31] If there are no torches to carry, four or six servers or other members of the faithful carrying hand candles could escort the celebrant.

[32] Cf. CMRR, no. 704. In some countries it is still customary to carry the

hand candles, customarily in their outside hands, including the laity, who immediately follow the celebrant. Those not taking part in the procession kneel as the Holy Eucharist passes them.[33]

212. When the procession reaches the Place of Reposition, the faithful remaining in their seats should turn towards this chapel or area. The cross bearer, candle bearers and thurifer(s) go to the right side of the area, where they remain standing facing across during the reposition of the Eucharist. Directed by the M.C., the choir, servers and clergy divide and form two or more lines, allowing the celebrant, deacon(s) and torch bearers to pass through. Facing in, they kneel as the celebrant arrives. Ushers guide the laity who took part in the procession.

213. The celebrant goes directly to the altar of repose and places the ciborium on the corporal. He genuflects, turns to his right and comes to the center of the area in front of the altar of repose. A server removes the humeral veil. Except for the cross bearer, candle bearers and thurifer(s), all kneel, and "Tantum ergo" is sung. At the end of the first verse, the thurifer approaches on the right of the celebrant, who, assisted by the deacon or M.C., prepares and blesses incense (in the first thurible). Then he kneels, bows, incenses the Eucharist with three double swings, bows once more and hands the thurible to the deacon or M.C. The celebrant remains kneeling. The thurifer takes the thurible and joins

canopy or baldachin during the procession on Holy Thursday, but this is not mentioned in the Missal or CLE.

[33] In some churches, all who do not take part in the procession remain kneeling while the Eucharist is transferred. This certainly enhances the sense of prayer, reverence and mystery. They should begin kneeling when the celebrant incenses the Eucharist *before* the procession and stand when the procession leaves the place of reposition.

the cross and candle bearers (and other thurifer) standing at the side.

214. All at the Place of Reposition and in the church remain kneeling when the deacon stands and goes to the altar of repose. He places the ciborium in the tabernacle of reposition, genuflects and locks the door. He returns to the celebrant and kneels. If there are no assisting clergy, the celebrant himself reposes the Eucharist. All remain kneeling in silent adoration for a time. Then, on a signal from the M.C., the celebrant and others who took part in the procession stand, genuflect,[34] and, led by the thurifer(s), cross and candle bearers, they return to the sacristy in silence. Laity who took part in the procession should remain for a time at the Place of Reposition. They could leave their hand candles burning there in a candelabra or sand tray.[35] Especially if the sacristy has become the "other place of reservation", strict silence must be observed there, as well as in the church.

215. Solemn adoration at the Place of Reposition should continue until midnight, and the faithful should be encouraged to maintain the "watch".[36] At midnight, the candles and lamps are extinguished and the flowers are removed, but one lamp should remain burning. A simpler form of adora-

---

[34] In countries where the episcopal conference has maintained the double genuflection, such as Australia, this act of reverence is customarily made now and whenever passing the Blessed Sacrament at the Place of Reposition.

[35] The candle stands from shrines may also be moved to the place of reposition so that the faithful may light their own "votive candles" there.

[36] Cf. CLE, no. 56, which commends the reflective reading of some part of John 13–17 during adoration. In some places it is customary to recite Compline before midnight. The pastor may terminate solemn adoration at an earlier hour, but only for serious reasons, and never forgetting that eucharistic adoration is a growing phenomenon of the Catholic revival. If the clergy cannot supervise the watch at the altar of repose, then adoration, even beyond midnight, should be entrusted to a well-organized lay group.

tion may, and should, continue throughout the early morning hours, even up to the Good Friday ceremonies, when this can be arranged.

The Bishop Presides at the Mass of the Lord's Supper

216. The concelebrated Mass follows the solemn pontifical form. The bishop wears the ornate miter, and he carries the crozier. At the Washing of the Feet, the bishop lays aside the miter and chasuble, but not the dalmatic, if he is wearing it. He may put on a linen gremial (or amice) as an apron. After Communion and during the Transfer of the Holy Eucharist, the skullcap is not worn, but the miter bearer keeps it with the miter. The procession follows the order described above, but the crozier bearer comes after the concelebrants. Two thurifers precede the bishop as he carries the Eucharist, and the book bearer and miter bearer follow him.[37] After the reposition of the Eucharist, the bishop puts on the skullcap and miter and takes the crozier for the silent procession from the place of reposition to the sacristy.

Stripping the Altars

217. After the Mass of the Lord's Supper and Transfer of the Holy Eucharist, commencing with the main altar, all the altars of the church are stripped and their candlesticks and crosses are removed.[38] Any portable crosses are removed from the church. Other crosses should be veiled in red or purple, unless they have already been veiled on the Saturday

---

[37] Cf. CB, no. 307.

[38] The stripping of the altars is to take place in silence, but in some places the former practice is still customary—reciting the antiphon "Dividunt . . ." and Psalm 21 while the clergy and servers strip the altars. According to a medieval custom, the mensa of each altar was washed with water and wine after the stripping, indicating that this is an opportunity for the sacristans to wash the altars.

before the Fifth Sunday in Lent.[39] This severe symbolism should extend to the whole church. Until the Gloria in the Easter Vigil, no candles or lamps burn elsewhere in the church, so lamps or votive lights must not be available at shrines or side altars. The sacristans remove all holy water from the stoups at the church doors. The stoups should also be cleaned. At Compline, the responsory is replaced by "Christ was made obedient. . . ."

On the night of that last supper,
Seated with his chosen band,
He the paschal victim eating
First fulfills the law's command;
Then, as food to his apostles,
Gives himself by his own hand.

Word made flesh, the bread of nature
By his word to flesh he turns;
Wine into his blood he changes:
What though sense no change discerns?
Only be the heart in earnest,
Faith her lesson quickly learns.

— from "Pange lingua",
Saint Thomas Aquinas

---

[39] Cf. MR, *Evening Mass of the Lord's Supper, Transfer of the Holy Eucharist*, no. 41; CLE, no. 57.

8.

Good Friday

218. We call "good" this day when Our Lord loved us and gave himself up for us, redeeming us from sin and death. Thus, while the liturgical rites of the day are austere, they are marked by the triumphant sign of Christ's Cross, and they glow with the color of his Precious Blood. The crowds who gather for the Good Friday liturgy are not only assistants at the Passion, expressing the human emotion of grief and mourning, but *Christian* men and women whose gift of faith in the one Redeemer and Savior gives them confidence and hope. The death of the Lord Jesus breaks open the Mystery of the Trinity; the God who is Love is revealed in the language and terms of a fallen world, that is, through rejection, pain and suffering. But at the heart of the Passion is the divine paradox: Death itself is put to death on this day which we call "good".

219. To meet the varied needs of the faithful in different pastoral situations, appropriate acts of worship for the morning of Good Friday could include the public celebration of the Office of Readings and Morning Prayer.[1] A more prolonged and solemn form of the Way of the Cross is appropriate. The Sacrament of Reconciliation should be available before, during and after all these celebrations. On this day confessions may, and should, be heard,[2] and the sick may be

---

[1] Cf. CLE, no. 62, and see appendix 7, "Tenebræ".

[2] Pope John Paul II has given the example here.

anointed, but, outside the liturgy, the Eucharist is only given to the sick or as Viaticum. The celebration of other sacraments is strictly forbidden. Funerals are celebrated without singing, music or the tolling of bells.[3] Vespers is recited only by those who do not participate in the Celebration of the Lord's Passion.

The Celebration of the Lord's Passion

220.   The Church gathers to celebrate the Passion and death of her Lord and Savior at the customary ninth hour, 3 P.M. The "lex orandi" of the liturgy underlines the historical reality of the event, which cuts across the whole of human history. In countries where Good Friday is not a public holiday, the Celebration may be celebrated earlier, for example, shortly after midday, or postponed to a later hour, in the evening, but not later than 9 P.M.[4] For good pastoral reasons the Celebration may even be repeated in the same church, for example, to accommodate large crowds.

221.   The Celebration of the Lord's Passion moves through three distinct stages: (1) the Liturgy of the Word, (2) the Veneration of the Cross and (3) Holy Communion. In the Liturgy of the Word the Passion of Saint John is read and the General Intercessions take the form of solemn public prayers for the Church and the world. The order of the Celebration of the Lord's Passion, which "stems from an ancient tradition of the Church, should be observed faithfully and religiously, and may not be changed by anyone on his own initiative."[5]

---

[3] Cf. CLE, no. 61.

[4] Cf. CLE, no. 59.

[5] CLE, no. 64, added in the light of experiments and attempts to change the order of the three distinct stages of the rite.

222. The celebrant should be assisted by a deacon. If there are two deacons, one assists at the Intercessions and the Veneration of the Cross and the other at the rite of Holy Communion. If there are no deacons, other priests present may assist the celebrant in these roles. If three deacons sing the Passion of Saint John, they wear red dalmatics over the alb and stole, or red stoles over the alb. Five well-trained servers suffice: two who will act later as the candle bearers, a book bearer and two others to assist as required. The cross for veneration is to be of "appropriate size and beauty",[6] usually a large and noble crucifix, so that the faithful may conveniently kiss the feet of the corpus. It is prepared in the sacristy or a side chapel. If the traditional form of showing the cross is to be observed, it is veiled in violet cloth, held by pins. The organ is played during the Celebration of the Lord's Passion only whenever it is required to sustain singing.

Immediate Preparations

223. *Altar*: bare, without any cloths or ornaments (carpets may also be removed from around the altar and on the sanctuary).

224. *Ambo*: Lectionary; no antependium; two lecterns may be set up on either side of the ambo for the reading of the Passion, or three bare lecterns may be set up later at the center of the sanctuary.

225. *Chair*: nearby, Missal or order of Holy Week.

226. *Credence table*: a bracket or stand for the cross with purifiers for the Veneration of the Cross; a neatly folded or rolled altar cloth, corporal, missal stand, a cruet of water and

---

[6] CLE, no. 68.

purifier(s), the ewer, basin and towel; vessel of water and purifier for those who distribute the Eucharist; empty ciboria or patens if required for Communion.

227. *Sanctuary*: a suitable stand or bracket for the cross, unless the bracket is only to be used to set it on the altar; books of the Passion of Saint John.

228. *Place of Reposition*: a corporal spread in front of the tabernacle, the key, red or white humeral veil; on or in front of the "altar of repose", two processional candlesticks with unlit candles, a taper to light them from the lamp.

229. *Sacristy*: red Mass vestments for the celebrant and deacons; alb and red stole, or choir dress and red stole for other priests and deacons; cross for veneration (veiled in violet), two processional candlesticks (if possible matching those at the Place of Reposition), unlit candles and matches (unless the cross and candles are prepared in a chapel or in the narthex). For those who read the Passion: albs, red stoles, and dalmatics if available, if they are deacons, or albs, if they are laity.

230. The faithful gather in silence; there is no singing and no music is played.[7] The procession enters in silence, in this order: servers (without cross or candles), a robed choir, lectors, clergy, other deacons who read the Passion, M.C., the deacon(s) and celebrant. On arriving at the sanctuary, all bow to the bare altar. Three servers go to their places at the credence table, the book bearer waits near the chair. Then the celebrant and deacon(s) prostrate themselves or kneel before the altar. This act of prostration, proper to the

---

[7] Any introductory words should be said *before* the clergy and servers enter; cf. CLE, no. 65. But this liturgy needs no introduction.

rite of the day, is to "be strictly observed".[8] While the sacred ministers are praying silently, all present should kneel in silent prayer. On a signal from the M.C., clergy, servers and congregation stand. Without kissing the altar, the celebrant and deacon(s) go to the chair. Attended by the book bearer, the celebrant sings or says the Opening Prayer, facing the people, hands extended.[9] He omits "let us pray", and there is no sign of the cross, greeting or introduction.

1. The Liturgy of the Word

231. All sit while the lectors proclaim the readings from Isaiah and Hebrews and the choir or cantor(s) sing the responsorial psalm. The readings are to be read in their entirety.[10] If the Reading of the Passion takes place at the ambo, and three books of the Passion reading are to be used, at the end of the second reading, the lector gives the Lectionary to a server, who takes it to the credence table. If they are not already in place, three bare lecterns are set up (with microphones, if necessary) at the center of the sanctuary or some other suitable and prominent place.

232. All stand for the sung acclamation before the Passion. The vested deacons or lectors come from their places in the sanctuary, each carrying a book of the Passion. Only deacons go to the celebrant at the chair to seek his blessing. They bow for his blessing as usual and then go directly to the lecterns and/or the ambo. The narrator stands at the central lectern (or ambo), Christus on his right, the crowd on his left. "The Lord be with you" and the signing of the

---

[8] CLE, no. 65, which adds "for it signifies both the abasement of the 'earthly man' and also the grief and sorrow of the Church".

[9] Cf. MR, *Good Friday*, no. 6.

[10] Cf. CLE, no. 66.

book are omitted.[11] As at Palm Sunday, the Passion should be sung, with the narrator and Christus and with the other reader and choir taking the parts of other characters and the crowd. If there is no deacon and the celebrant reads the Passion, he takes the part of Christ. All stand during the Passion.[12] After the verse recounting the death of Our Lord, all kneel in silent prayer for a few moments. Those reading the Passion kneel facing the lecterns or ambo. At the end of the reading, "(This is) the Gospel of the Lord" is sung or said, but the book is not kissed. Those who read the Passion take up their books, come before the altar, bow to it and return to their places. The lecterns are removed by servers. A homily follows, but it should be brief, to allow the Passion of Saint John to speak for itself. The faithful may be invited to spend a short time in meditation after the homily.[13]

233.   At the chair,[14] attended by the book bearer, the celebrant introduces the General Intercessions, which are "to follow the wording and form handed down by ancient tradition".[15] Ten intentions are provided, each consisting of an invitation to prayer, a time for silent prayer and a prayer sung or said by the celebrant, hands extended. The celebrant may select the intentions that are more appropriate to local circumstances from among the ten provided, but always maintain-

---

[11] Cf. CB, no. 273; MR, *Good Friday*, no. 9.

[12] The elderly and mothers with small children may be advised to sit; otherwise standing for the Passion should be maintained, especially on this day.

[13] Cf. CLE, no. 66.

[14] Or at the altar or even at the ambo; cf. MR, *Good Friday*, no. 11. It seems preferable to preside over the prayers from the chair, but if they are said at the altar, the book bearer brings the missal stand and Missal or order of Holy Week to the altar immediately after the homily.

[15] CLE, no. 67, "maintaining the full range of intentions, so as to signify clearly the universal effect of the Passion of Christ. . . ."

ing the essential prayers for the Church and the world.[16] The deacon(s) or lectors may proclaim the introductions at the ambo.[17] The people kneel for the time of silent prayer, but they may remain kneeling or standing for all the Intercessions. The episcopal conference may indicate an antiphon to be sung by the people before the priest's prayer, or the conference may decree that the deacon's traditional invitation "Let us kneel" and "Let us stand" be sung or said,[18] to call the assembly to kneel in silent prayer before standing for the celebrant's prayer.

234. At the conclusion of the General Intercessions, all sit while preparations are made for the Veneration of the Cross. In some places, the annual collection for the Holy Places is taken up now, but there should be no singing or music.

2. *The Veneration of the Cross*

235. The rite of venerating the cross "should be carried out with the splendour worthy of the mystery of our salvation".[19] There are two options for the showing of the cross before the Veneration, the traditional gradual unveiling of the cross, or showing the cross, already unveiled, during a procession through the church. Pastoral needs and the local situation will guide the pastor in discerning which option is more effective.[20] However, in practice, the unveiling of the cross in the first option can easily be combined with the procession in the second.

---

[16] In times of serious public need the Ordinary may permit or decree other intentions; cf. MR, *Good Friday*, no. 12; CLE, no. 67.

[17] Cf. CB, no. 320.

[18] Cf. MR, *Good Friday*, no. 12. Even if it is not decreed by the conference, this preferable practice can be chosen by the celebrant.

[19] CLE, no. 68.

[20] Cf. MR, *Good Friday*, no. 14.

236. *1. Showing and unveiling the cross.* Preceded by the candle bearers (without candles), the deacon or, lacking a deacon, the celebrant goes to the sacristy or place where the veiled cross for veneration has been prepared. The candle bearers light the processional candles that have been prepared there. The deacon or celebrant takes the veiled cross and, flanked by the candle bearers, carries it reverently to the altar. All stand as he enters the church or the sanctuary.[21] At the altar the celebrant receives the cross from the deacon, who then stands on his right. The candle bearers flank the celebrant, facing one another. A server waits near the altar to take the veil after the third showing of the cross. The book bearer may assist, holding the Missal, order of Holy Week or a card with the text and music on it. Facing the people the celebrant first unveils the top of the cross, but not the face of the corpus. Then he raises it high while singing, "Ecce lignum Crucis . . ." (This is the wood of the cross . . .). The deacon, a cantor or the choir may sing these words or accompany the celebrant, for they are meant to be sung.[22] The assembly responds by singing, "Venite adoremus" (Come, let us worship), and, except for the celebrant and candle bearers, all kneel and venerate the cross in silence. This procedure is repeated for the unveiling of the right arm and then of the whole corpus.[23] A server takes the veil to the credence table after the celebrant has sung "Ecce lignum Crucis" for a third time.

237. Flanked by the candle bearers, the celebrant takes the cross to the center of the sanctuary, where he places it in a bracket

---

[21] It would seem best to bring it from the sacristy or some other place to the main door and then carry it through the body of the church as for the second option.

[22] Cf. CLE, no. 68. Traditionally, "Ecce lignum Crucis . . ." (This is the wood of the cross) is sung three times in an ascending pitch.

[23] Cf. MR, *Good Friday*, no. 15.

or on a stand. The other two servers bring purifiers to wipe the feet of the corpus, if it is to be kissed. The candle bearers place their candles on the pavement on each side of the cross. If a bracket is not used, the other two servers hold the cross, one on each side, but in such a way as to assist the faithful who wish to kiss the feet of the corpus.[24]

238.   2. *Showing the cross during a procession.* Preceded by the candle bearers (without candles), the deacon or, lacking a deacon, the celebrant goes to the entrance of the church or narthex, where the cross for veneration has been prepared. The candle bearers light the processional candles. The deacon or celebrant takes the cross and, flanked by the candle bearers, carries it reverently into the church. All stand as he enters the church. Near the entrance of the church he stops, raises the cross high and sings, "Ecce lignum Crucis . . ." (This is the wood of the cross). The assembly responds by singing, "Venite adoremus" (Come, let us worship). Then, except for the deacon or celebrant carrying the cross and the candle bearers, all kneel and venerate the cross in silence.[25] The procession slowly continues, and this procedure is repeated at the middle of the church and finally at the entrance to the sanctuary, where the deacon or celebrant may turn to the people as he raises the cross. Then the cross is placed in the bracket or stand with the candles on each side of it, as described in the preceding paragraph.

239.   The choir and cantor(s) now sing the Antiphon, the Reproaches, the hymn "Pange lingua gloriosi prœlium certaminis" and other appropriate hymns.[26] The celebrant goes

---

[24] In some places, the cross is placed on a large cushion on a small table or frame, with an inclined angle, so that it is easier to kiss the feet of the corpus.

[25] Cf. MR, *Good Friday*, no. 16.

[26] Indicated in MR, *Good Friday, Songs at the Veneration of the Cross*, with provision for "some other suitable songs" in CB, no. 322, and CLE, no. 69.

to the chair, where, assisted by the deacon or M.C., he removes the chasuble.[27] With the deacon(s), he returns to the
center of the sanctuary to lead the procession for the Veneration of the Cross. This procession may well begin in the
main aisle of the church. The celebrant leads, followed by
the deacon(s), other priests and deacons, the M.C., servers
and members of the faithful. The celebrant genuflects to
the cross, and then he may, and should, come to the cross
and kiss the feet of the corpus. He returns to the chair and
puts on the chasuble. The clergy, servers and members of
the faithful follow the same procedure, according to local
custom.[28] Having venerated the cross, the servers take turns
wiping the feet of the corpus with purifiers after each person
has kissed them. During the Veneration, a server brings a
smaller bracket or stand and places it at the center of the
altar—unless the larger one used at the veneration will be
placed there.

240.   Only *one* cross is to be venerated, because the act of personal veneration is the most important feature in this celebration. It will take time, but "taking time" is essential to
Good Friday. Only if there are very large numbers of the
faithful present should the rite of veneration be made simultaneously by all present.[29]

241.   This simultaneous veneration is carried out as follows. After
some of the clergy, servers and representatives of the faithful
have venerated the cross, the celebrant may go to the altar,

Organ music or other instrumental music should only serve as accompaniment,
if necessary. A skilled choir could well draw on the various settings for the Latin
and Greek texts of the *Improperia*.
    [27] Cf. CB, no. 322, and following the option offered to the bishop, he may
also remove his shoes.
    [28] Cf. MR, *Good Friday*, no. 18; CB, no. 322.
    [29] CLE, no. 69.

where he receives the cross brought by the deacon. Lacking a deacon, the celebrant takes the cross from its bracket himself and goes up to the altar. Standing in front of the altar, facing the people, he invites the assembly to venerate the cross together with a few appropriate words. Then, for some moments, he holds it up for them to venerate in silence, meaning that all present should kneel in silent prayer for some moments.[30]

242. After the Veneration of the Cross, flanked by the candle bearers with the candles, the deacon or, lacking a deacon, the celebrant carries the cross to the altar. He is followed by a server carrying the bracket or stand, unless one has already been placed on the altar. The other server takes the soiled purifiers to the credence table. The deacon/celebrant places the cross in the bracket or stand on the altar at the center, with the corpus facing the people. The candle bearers place their candles on, beside, or in front of the altar, as may be convenient, but flanking the cross. The celebrant and deacon go to the chair and sit. The book bearer and the other server go to the credence table.

3. Holy Communion

243. All sit while the altar is prepared for Holy Communion. The folded or rolled cloth is brought from the credence table and carefully spread over the mensa by a server.[31] Then a server brings the corporal and unfolds it at the center of the altar. The book bearer brings the missal stand with the

---

[30] Cf. MR, *Good Friday*, no. 19; CB, no. 323. All kneeling in silent prayer for some moments is the current practice at Saint Peter's Basilica, Rome.

[31] But if the cloth covers the whole of the mensa, the server should spread it just *before* the cross is brought to the altar, if the stand or bracket will rest on the cloth. In some churches the bracket, cross and candles are arranged along the back of the mensa so that the rite of Communion may be celebrated facing the apse, that is, towards the crucifix.

Missal or order of Holy Week and arranges it to the left of the corporal. If necessary, another server puts a microphone on the altar. Meanwhile, the deacon/celebrant goes to the Place of Reposition, preceded by the candle bearers, carrying nothing.[32] They genuflect to the Blessed Sacrament. Assisted by the first candle bearer the deacon/celebrant puts on the humeral veil. Using a taper, the second candle bearer lights the processional candles from the lamp. The candle bearers take up the candles and stand facing the "altar of repose". The deacon/celebrant opens the tabernacle, genuflects, places the ciborium on the corporal and arranges it under the humeral veil. Preceded by the candle bearers carrying processional candles, the deacon/celebrant slowly returns to the sanctuary.

244. All stand as the Blessed Sacrament is brought in silence from the Place of Reposition.[33] If more vessels containing the Eucharist are to be brought from the other place of reservation, this is done now without any ceremony, and those who brought these vessels wait near the altar, holding the vessels. On arriving at the sanctuary, the candle bearers go directly to the altar and simultaneously place their candles on or next to it. Once the Blessed Sacrament has been placed on the altar, they genuflect together and join the other servers near the credence table.

245. After the deacon/celebrant has placed the ciborium on the corporal, he uncovers it, genuflects and steps back. The M.C. or server removes the humeral veil, which the server

---

[32] An instituted acolyte or another extraordinary minister does not carry the Eucharist in this procession from the Place of Reposition, but such assistants may be needed to bring other vessels containing the Eucharist directly from "the other place of reservation".

[33] In order to underline the simple action, it may be best to move through the body of the church.

takes to the credence table. Other vessels containing the Blessed Sacrament are now brought to the altar by clergy or extraordinary ministers, and the deacon/celebrant receives them and arranges them, uncovered, on the corporal. If necessary, Hosts from the main ciborium and other vessels are placed in empty ciboria and patens brought from the credence table by the servers. If he is not already there, the celebrant comes to the altar and genuflects. The deacon stands on his right, back a few paces (a second deacon stands on his left).

246. With joined hands, the celebrant sings the introduction to the Lord's Prayer. He extends his hands, and all sing the Lord's Prayer. He sings or says the embolism, "Deliver us, Lord, . . .", hands extended, and the acclamation, "For the kingdom . . ." follows as usual. But the sign of peace is not given on Good Friday.[34] Then the celebrant, with joined hands, quietly says, "Lord Jesus Christ, with faith . . ." (Perceptio corporis). He genuflects, takes a Host, and holding it above the ciborium, which he raises slightly with his left hand, he says, "This is the Lamb of God. . . ." All respond, "Lord I am not worthy. . . ." He receives the Host, saying quietly "May the Body of Christ. . . ." He gives Communion first to the deacon(s), then to priests and other deacons present, the servers and the faithful. As required, the deacon(s), other clergy and, where necessary, acolytes and other extraordinary ministers assist in distributing Holy Communion to the faithful. Appropriate hymns, psalms, motets, etc., may be sung by the choir and people during Communion, but the organ is only played to accompany singing when necessary.

---

[34] Cf. CLE, no. 70. The sign of peace is obviously linked to the Resurrection, for the first word of the risen Lord is "Shalom!" (cf. John 20:19 and 21).

247. After Communion, the deacon, celebrant or another priest places the Hosts from other vessels in the ciborium, as required. Without ceremony, apart from the usual genuflections, the Blessed Sacrament is now taken by deacon(s), assisting priest(s), acolyte(s) or other extraordinary minister(s) directly to the *other* place of reservation. Under normal circumstances, the Eucharist should not be put in the main tabernacle or taken back to the Place of Reposition. Empty ciboria or patens are taken to the credence table, where a deacon, assisting priest, instituted acolyte or, if necessary, the celebrant purifies them with water, which he consumes. A server folds the corporal and takes it to the credence table. The Missal and stand remain on the altar. The candle bearers bring the ewer, basin and towel to the celebrant at the altar or seated at the chair,[35] and he washes his hands, unless he has already cleansed them at the altar or the credence table using a finger bowl and purifier. Others who distributed Holy Communion cleanse their hands as usual at a credence table.

248. A period of silence may now be observed. Then, on a signal from the M.C., all stand. If they are not already there, the celebrant and deacon(s) go to the altar. The celebrant says "Let us pray" and the Prayer after Communion, hands extended. Then, facing the people, he extends his hands towards them and says the Prayer over the People, which serves as the dismissal.[36] He closes the Missal or order of Holy Week. Without kissing the altar, he comes to the cen-

---

[35] CB, nos. 328 and 329, make no reference to the bishop returning to the cathedra, but the M.C. may decide it is more convenient for the celebrant to return to the chair while others carry out the purifications and rearrange the altar.

[36] Cf. MR, *Good Friday*, no. 31. The final prayers are not sung, nor is the celebrant to add anything at this point.

ter of the sanctuary with the deacon(s), joining the M.C. and the servers. All genuflect to the cross and return to the sacristy or vesting room in silent procession, in the same order as for the entrance. After the Celebration of the Lord's Passion, silence should be observed not only in the church but in the sacristy. However, priests should make themselves available for confessions immediately after the Good Friday Liturgy, because this is a time when casual or fallen-away Catholics are drawn back to Christ and his Church.

249. After the Celebration of the Lord's Passion, the servers remove everything from the altar, so that it is bare. The cross is taken to an appropriate place such as the chapel or area used for reposition on Holy Thursday or some other chapel, where it remains in its bracket, with the four candles used during the liturgy burning near it. Here "the faithful may venerate and kiss it, and spend some time in meditation."[37] However, no candles or lamps burn elsewhere in the church on Good Friday, so votive lights must not be available at shrines. On the evening of Good Friday a form of Tenebræ,[38] the Stations of the Cross or popular devotions or processions of the Passion or commemorations in honor of the Mother of Sorrows may be celebrated according to custom. These devotions should be set for a time that makes it clear "that the liturgical celebration by its very nature surpasses them in importance."[39] At Compline, the responsory is replaced by "Christ was made obedient. . . ."

---

[37] CLE, no. 71; also a useful provision for those unable to take part in the afternoon celebration.

[38] See appendix 7, "Tenebræ".

[39] CLE, no. 72.

*The Bishop Presides at the
Celebration of the Lord's Passion*

250. On Good Friday, the bishop wears the simple miter, but he does not use the crozier, nor does he wear the ring.[40] When he venerates the cross, he lays aside the miter, skullcap, and the chasuble, and he may remove his shoes.[41] If he assists in choir dress, he may preside at the Communion Rite, after removing his skullcap and putting a red stole and cope over his rochet. If he does not choose to preside at Communion, having put on a red stole, he comes to the altar and waits until the celebrant has received the Eucharist. The celebrant steps to one side, the bishop genuflects, takes a Host from the ciborium or paten and gives himself the Eucharist.[42]

Holy Saturday

251. The Church waits at the tomb of Jesus Christ. On this day of prayer and fasting, the austerity of Lent and Passiontide reaches the point of emptiness and desolation. Our Lord has descended to the dead. As we wait in hope for his Resurrection, the rites of Holy Saturday are simple and express a mood of preparation and anticipation.

252. Mass is never celebrated on Holy Saturday. The Eucharist is only given as Viaticum. Penance and the Anointing of the Sick can be celebrated on this day. But the celebration of Marriage is forbidden, pastoral "pressure" notwithstanding.[43] The crucifix venerated on Good Friday may remain

---

[40] Cf. CB, no. 315 a; signifying the spiritual widowhood of the Church on this day when we fast because the Bridegroom is no longer with us.
[41] Cf. CB, no. 322.
[42] Cf. CB, no. 327.
[43] Cf. CLE, no. 75.

in its bracket in the place of reposition or an appropriate chapel. An image of the dead Christ or of his descent to the dead or of the Mother of Sorrows may also be set up for the devotion of the faithful.[44] It is highly recommended that the Office of Readings and Morning Prayer be celebrated, perhaps as Tenebræ or, if this is not possible, a Liturgy of the Word or a para-liturgy.[45] Violet copes and/or stoles are worn at such celebrations, which may appropriately take place before or after confessions, or even during confessions when there are many penitents and enough clergy are available. If, in accord with civil laws, a funeral has to be celebrated on this day, it should be simple, without bells or music.

253. If the Christian Initiation of Adults is to be celebrated at the Easter Vigil, the anointing with the Oil of Catechumens and the recitation of the Creed may be combined as a rite of immediate preparation, as noted above. For the sake of convenience this rite should take place well before the Easter Vigil, either during a simple Liturgy of the Word or as a simple celebration for catechumens and their sponsors, that is, in the context of the final instruction and preparation of the elect for their Baptism and Confirmation.

254. On this day, the sacristans and others directed by them clean, adorn and prepare the church for the splendor of the Easter Vigil. However, to accentuate the coming Vigil, candles or lamps do not burn in the church on Holy Saturday, thus, as on Good Friday, votive lights must not be available at shrines. In the evening, the altars are dressed with the finest antependia and cloths, and the candles, flowers and ornaments are set up for the Easter Vigil. Where the custom of veiling images has been observed, the violet veils are

---

[44] Cf. CLE, no. 74.
[45] Cf. CLE, no. 73, and see appendix 7, "Tenebræ".

now removed from all crosses and images. Those who take part in the Easter Vigil recite Vespers of Holy Saturday, but Compline for Holy Saturday and the Office of Readings for Easter Day are recited only by those who do not participate in the Vigil.

When he had seen the sun's rays hidden and the temple veil torn asunder while the Savior died, Joseph went to Pilate and cried:

> Give me that Stranger,
> who had wandered since his youth as a stranger.
> Give me that Stranger,
> by hatred slain, as a stranger.
> Give me that Stranger,
> whom I behold with wonder, seeing him a guest of death.
> Give me that Stranger,
> cut off from this world by envious men.
> Give me that Stranger,
> that I might lay him in a tomb,
> who, being a stranger, has no place to rest his head.
> Give me that Stranger,
> to whom his Mother cried when she saw him dead:
> "My Son, wounded are my senses and my heart burns as I behold you dead!
> Yet I praise you, for I trust in your Resurrection!"

— Byzantine Troparion of the Burial of Christ

9.

The Easter Vigil

255. This is the high point of the Christian year, the celebration of the Paschal Mystery in the great Easter Eucharist, summit and source of the liturgical action and life of God's People. This "holy night" is the "mother of all holy vigils" that begins the "queen of feasts". The full meaning of the Easter Vigil is a waiting for the Lord.[1] He who took our human flesh, who suffered and died for us in that flesh, now rises in that same human body, glorified and immortal, as befits the new life of Resurrection. With the joyous "alleluias" of her new Passover, Mother Church celebrates a unique event, at once historical and cosmic. At the broken tomb, the Incarnation reaches its fulfillment, and the ultimate purpose of our Redemption is revealed in the frailty of human flesh—nothing less than a literal sharing in the glory of his bodily Resurrection. For this we were washed by the waters of Baptism; for this we were sealed with the Spirit's fragrant Chrism; for this we feast on the Body and Blood of the One who leads us on into eternal life.

256. The solemn Vigil and first Mass of Easter are celebrated only once in the same church.[2] The Easter Vigil takes place at night, never beginning before nightfall and always ending before daybreak on Sunday. "This rule is to be taken

---

[1] Cf. CLE, no. 80.

[2] It could be divisive to provide a second separate celebration in the *same* church for any special group.

according to its strictest sense."³ The sacraments of Christian Initiation should be celebrated where possible, at least in the form of the Baptism of Infants. The greatest exterior solemnity should be lavished on the Vigil Mass. The music should be carefully prepared to express joy, festivity and the triumph of the risen Lord.

257. The celebration of the Easter Vigil moves through four distinctive stages: (1) the Solemn Beginning of the Vigil: the Service of Light; (2) Liturgy of the Word; (3) Liturgy of Baptism; and (4) Liturgy of the Eucharist. "This liturgical order must not be changed by anyone on his own initiative."⁴

258. The *Easter candle* or *Paschal candle* is the central symbolic object in the celebration of the Vigil liturgy because it represents the risen Lord in his glory. This candle should be made of fine quality wax, preferably pure beeswax. Only one candle is prepared. It should be a new candle made for each year, not last year's candle recycled, and never part of a candle mounted on a false candle or an artificial candle (a canister of fuel concealed in a plastic "candle").⁵ It should be large, but not to the extent of being too heavy for one person to carry. The decoration of the candle varies according to the local culture, but the finest Easter candles are adorned with colored wax or hand painted. However, the decoration should not obscure or detract from the principal symbols: (1) space for a cross to be incised in the wax, (2) five points

---

³ CLE, no. 78. This circular letter on Easter condemns making the time of the vigil coincide with the time of the normal Saturday evening Mass for Sunday, that is, when this begins before sunset. In timing the Vigil, daylight saving time should also be taken into account.

⁴ CLE, no. 81, and see Peter J. Elliott, *Liturgical Question Box*, "Rearranging the Easter Vigil", (San Francisco: Ignatius Press, 1998), pp. 178–79.

⁵ See CLE, no. 82.

where the "grains of incense" are inserted, (3) space for the date, preferably set within the four quarters of the cross, and (4) above the cross, the Greek capital Alpha (A) and, below it, the Greek capital Omega (Ω).[6] The "grains of incense" should be significant objects, made of any suitable material, equipped with a sharp pin to ensure they hold fast in the wax.[7]

259. The candlestick for the Easter candle should be a truly noble object. It may be adorned with flowers, foliage or rich fabric. This candlestick is placed near the ambo or the altar or, at least during the Vigil rites, even at the center of the sanctuary. If it is very high, a secure set of wooden steps should be provided so that the candle can easily be placed in it and later removed for the baptismal rites.[8] A low stand seems inappropriate at the Vigil, although outside the Easter Season, it may be found more practical to set the Easter candle in a lower candlestick or bracket near the font.

260. The "new fire" of Easter at the gathering place should be a large bonfire, "whose flames should be such that they genuinely dispel the darkness and light up the night".[9] Depending on local circumstances, and taking safety into account, ushers or other laity prepare, maintain and supervise the fire. After the procession with the Easter candle has entered the church, and the faithful have lit their candles,

---

[6] The modern rite leaves open the option to dispense with some of these signs, but this would rob the candle of a richer symbolism and accessible meaning.

[7] If literal "grains of incense" are preferred to brass ones, these can be made by gently warming some incense and molding it into a ball around the head of a large pin. Each grain may then be painted or, better still, gilded. Before the Vigil, the sacristan should ensure that five holes are prepared in the wax for the grains.

[8] Before the ceremonies, the sacristan must ensure that the candle fits easily and securely into the socket.

[9] CLE, no. 82.

those in charge of the new fire should remain at the gathering place and carefully extinguish the fire before entering the church themselves.

261. Everything is prepared for a Solemn Mass, with deacon(s), concelebrants and M.C., and the full complement of servers: cross and candle bearers, thurifer(s), book bearer, two, four or six torch bearers. This is an occasion when a second M.C. is useful, especially to supervise the concelebrants, lectors and candidates and sponsors for Baptism. Where the Mass takes a less solemn form, without a deacon, an M.C. should direct the ceremonies, and at least four servers should assist as thurifer, candle bearers and book bearer. The exact duties of all the servers, sacristans and ushers must be clearly assigned to them by the M.C. before the ceremonies. For convenience, the main duties have been assigned below to the first and second candle bearers ("acolytes"). Other duties may be given to those who will later act as torch bearers during the Mass. If the deacon and the celebrant do not have adequate vocal skills, a lay cantor vested in an alb may sing the Exsultet. Well-prepared lectors read the Old Testament prophecies and the Epistle of the Mass.

262. If the sacraments of Christian Initiation are to be celebrated, candidates and sponsors, or parents and godparents, must be instructed and prepared beforehand so that they can participate without hesitation or confusion. It would be best if they were accompanied by a well-trained guide or even another M.C.

Immediate Preparations

263. *Altar:* Six or four unlit candles, in the best candlesticks; (the best white or cloth of gold/silver antependium); flowers according to local custom; the (unveiled) processional crucifix near the altar, or in another convenient place if it is not the

altar crucifix, the Book of the Gospels in its noblest cover, closed, on the altar.

264. *Ambo*: the candlestick for the Easter candle to one side, unless it is placed at the center of the sanctuary; the book of the Exsultet, open, and, nearby, the Lectionary, marked for the prophecies and other readings, lector's text of the General Intercessions (the best white or cloth of gold/silver antependium).

265. *Baptistery or at a convenient place in or near the sanctuary*: the font filled with water or a large vessel of water, perhaps adorned with flowers, or covered with fine fabric if it is not a noble vessel in itself, an empty holy water bucket and sprinkler, convenient jug(s) for transferring water. If Baptism is to be administered: the vessel for pouring water, Sacred Chrism, lemon and/or soap, and a jug or ewer of warm water, basin and towel, other towels as required, white robes for infants or adults, baptismal candle(s). If an immersion font is to be blessed, this is filled with water, and flowers and/or sweet-smelling herbs may be arranged around it.

266. *Credence table*: the finest eucharistic vessels, Missal and stand, ewer, bowl and towel, bell and any other bells to be rung at the Gloria, the two processional candlesticks with unlit candles, several tapers. If the sacraments of Christian Initiation are to be celebrated: the volume of the Roman Ritual for the RCIA or Baptism of Infants and a list of the candidates. If Confirmation will be given in the sanctuary: Sacred Chrism, gremial veil or amice (if the celebrant sits to confirm), lemon and/or soap and a ewer of warm water, basin and towel.

267. *Table of gifts*: bread, wine and water for the procession of the gifts.

268. *Tabernacle*: empty, open, the key, the best white or cloth of gold/silver veil nearby, the lamp(s) prepared, but unlit.

269. *In the church*: If the sacraments of Christian Initiation are to be celebrated, places are reserved for the catechumens and their sponsors or for the infants and their families. A faldstool or suitable chair is prepared at one side, if the celebrant sits to confirm. In a dedicated church, unlit candles are placed at the twelve or four consecration crosses. According to custom, not only the sanctuary but side altars and shrines are adorned with flowers and unlit candles and lamps, and supplies of votive lights are available. The holy water stoups at the doors are clean and empty.

270. *Sacristy*: the finest white or cloth of gold/silver eucharistic vestments for the celebrant and deacon(s) and all other requirements for a Solemn Mass; hand candles for concelebrants, clergy and servers who do not carry another object to the gathering place, (tray with the objects required for preparing the candle), a torch, Missal or order of Holy Week.

271. *Gathering place*: The new fire is kindled and carefully supervised so as to be blazing at the beginning of the rite. Unless brought on a tray by a server, the following are arranged on a small table: the stylus for marking the wax, the five "grains of incense", a taper or thin candle (preferably attached to a long metal tube), some charcoal pellets for incense and tongs. Hand candles and books or booklets for the liturgy are distributed to all the faithful as they gather.

272. If it is not possible to light the new fire outside the church, a small brazier may be prepared in the porch or narthex or some other suitable area.[10] The people gather in the church,

---

[10] Every effort should be made to avoid using a portable barbeque.

and hand candles are distributed. Because the initial rites take place at the back of the church, the faithful turn to face that area until the procession goes to the sanctuary.

1. Solemn Beginning of the Vigil: The Service of Light

273. The lights in the church are extinguished by the usher designated to supervise lighting. Except for those physically unable to take part in the procession, people already in the church should be encouraged to go to the gathering place.[11] Ushers ensure that the people take positions on each side of the fire, while allowing ample space for the procession to come from the church. By now, everyone at the gathering place should have an unlit hand candle and a booklet for the rites. At the chosen hour, the sacred ministers and servers leave the sacristy or vesting room and go in silence to the gathering place in this order: thurifer with an empty thurible and boat, robed choir,[12] the first candle bearer carrying the unlit Easter candle, other servers, book bearer, clergy in choir dress, concelebrants, M.C., deacon(s) and celebrant. Clergy and servers not carrying an object bring an unlit hand candle. The book bearer brings the Missal or the order of Holy Week; another server brings a flashlight.

BLESSING OF THE FIRE AND LIGHTING OF THE CANDLE

274. Directed by the M.C., the clergy and servers take positions so that the fire is between them and the church. The celebrant stands facing the fire, the deacon stands on the

---

[11] However, if Christian Initiation will be celebrated, it would seem best for catechumens and their sponsors to remain in the dark church. Moreover, the catechumens ought not to carry hand candles at this stage, because they will later receive the "light of Christ" at their Baptism.

[12] A choir without robes would already be with the faithful at the gathering place.

celebrant's right, the book bearer assists on his left. To the celebrant's right (where the table may be set up), the M.C. supervises the thurifer and other servers who stand in a line behind the celebrant. Concelebrants and clergy in choir dress stand in two lines on each side of the fire. The choir takes a convenient place so as to be able to join the faithful in the procession. Everyone at the gathering place keeps a reasonable distance from the fire.

275. Attended by the book bearer and the server directing the light of the flashlight onto the text, the celebrant makes the sign of the cross and greets the assembly, using one of the formulas at the beginning of Mass. Then the celebrant (or a deacon or concelebrant) introduces the rite, using the text provided or similar words. The celebrant sings or says, "Let us pray", and, after a pause for silent prayer, he sings or says the prayer of blessing, hands joined. He makes the sign of the cross over the fire at "make this new fire holy." Now, while the candle is being prepared, a server (or the boat bearer) carefully lights a taper from the fire and goes around behind the celebrant and deacon to prepare the thurible. Another server takes each of the charcoal pellets in the tongs and holds it over the taper. When each pellet is properly kindled, he places it in the thurible, which is held open by the thurifer.

276. *Preparation of the Easter candle*: The first candle bearer brings the Easter candle to the celebrant, standing directly in front of him and holding it securely at a convenient angle, assisted if necessary by the M.C. or another server. A server brings the tray with the stylus and incense grains and stands in front of the celebrant, on his right, or the second candle bearer brings these objects from the table as they are needed. He first presents the stylus to the celebrant, who marks the candle, saying "Christ yesterday and today" as he traces the

vertical arm of the cross, "the beginning and the end", as he traces the horizontal arm of the cross, then "Alpha" above the cross, "Omega" below the cross, and "all time belongs to him", inserting the first numeral of the year in the upper left corner of the cross, "and all the ages", inserting the second numeral of the year in the upper right corner, "to him be glory and power", inserting the third numeral in the lower left corner, and "through every age for ever. Amen", inserting the last numeral in the lower right corner.[13] The server receives the stylus from the celebrant. Then he gives the celebrant the five "grains of incense", one at a time. The celebrant takes the first grain and inserts it firmly at the top of the vertical arm, saying "By his holy"; he inserts the second at the center, saying "and glorious wounds", the third at the base of the vertical arm, saying "may Christ our Lord", the fourth at the left end of the horizontal arm, saying, "guard us" and the fifth at the right end of the horizontal arm, saying "and keep us. Amen."[14]

277. The Easter candle bearer holds the candle upright. The deacon or M.C. takes the taper (attached to the tube) and carefully lights it from the fire. He hands it to the celebrant who carefully lights the Easter candle, saying clearly "May the light of Christ . . . hearts and minds". The book bearer steps aside and closes the Missal or order of Holy Week. The thurifer approaches, and, assisted by the deacon, the celebrant prepares incense for the procession. Then the deacon or, lacking a deacon, the celebrant takes the Easter candle; directed by the M.C., he moves to a position where he will lead the procession into the church. If the deacon assists, the M.C. gives a hand candle to the celebrant.

---

[13] Cf. MR, *Easter Vigil*, no. 11; CB, no. 314.

[14] Cf. MR, *Easter Vigil*, no. 12. The episcopal conference may introduce other rites that may be better adapted to the local culture; see also CB, no. 341.

THE PROCESSION

278. The order of the procession is as follows: the thurifer precedes the deacon or celebrant who carries the Easter candle, then follow the celebrant (and second deacon), the M.C., concelebrants, other clergy, candle bearers without candles, other servers, book bearer, the choir and the faithful. At the church door, the procession pauses, and, facing the door, the deacon/celebrant raises the candle high and sings "Lumen Christi" (Christ our light). Led by the choir or cantors, all respond "Deo gratias" (Thanks be to God).[15] Care should be taken to protect the Easter candle from drafts of air at the church door. The deacon lowers the candle, and the celebrant lights his candle from it. Then the deacon/celebrant leads the procession as far as the center of the church, where he stops, raises the candle high and sings "Lumen Christi" (Christ our light) a second time. All respond "Deo gratias" (Thanks be to God). Servers take light from the Easter candle, using tapers or their own hand candles, and light the candles of those in the procession. The light is passed back so that all the hand candles are gradually lit. The procession continues to the sanctuary. The deacon/celebrant enters the sanctuary, turns to face the people, raises the candle high and sings "Lumen Christi" (Christ our light) a third time. All respond "Deo gratias" (Thanks be to God).

279. The deacon/celebrant places the Easter candle in its candlestick, either at the center of the sanctuary or next to the ambo or altar. The celebrant bows to the altar and goes

---

[15] In some places the more melodious Latin original is used because the vernacular text is not particularly suitable for singing. However, the episcopal conference may provide another richer acclamation; cf. MR, *Easter Vigil*, no. 14. CLE, no. 83, allows "some acclamation in honor of Christ" to be added to "Thanks be to God."

directly to the chair, with the M.C. The deacon joins him there. Concelebrants, clergy, servers and choir bow to the altar and go to their places. Ushers guide the faithful to their places in the church. There is no music during or after the procession. The lights of the church are supposed to be switched on at this point, but in practice it seems much better to defer this until after the Exsultet and, where possible, to increase the light gradually until the church is fully illuminated at the Gloria.

THE EASTER PROCLAMATION (EXSULTET)

280. The thurifer goes to the chair, where, assisted by the deacon, the celebrant prepares and blesses incense as usual. The thurifer waits to one side, facing the celebrant. The deacon asks for the celebrant's blessing and is blessed with an adapted form of the blessing before the Gospel.[16] Preceded by the thurifer, the deacon goes to the ambo. He takes the thurible and first incenses the book of the Exsultet with three double swings, as if it were the Book of the Gospels. Then he walks around the Easter candle, while incensing it with three double swings.[17] He gives the thurible back to the thurifer and returns to the ambo to sing the Exsultet.[18] A server with the flashlight may assist him if the light is inadequate. All present remain standing for the Exsultet, holding their hand candles.[19] The thurifer remains near the

---

[16] See MR, *Easter Vigil*, no. 18. If the Missal or order of Holy Week is used for the Exsultet, the book bearer hands this volume to the deacon as soon as he has been blessed by the celebrant, and the deacon takes it to the ambo. After the Exsultet, the book bearer retrieves it from the ambo.

[17] Cf. CB, no. 92 and custom.

[18] Singing the Exsultet requires not only skill but a sense of the rhythm of the music and words. It is not meant to be slow or heavy, but rather sustained by a subtle light and joyous style.

[19] The people may sing acclamations at various points during the Exsultet if

ambo, swinging the thurible moderately at full length until the end of the Exsultet.

281.   If there is no deacon and the celebrant sings the Exsultet, he prepares incense and follows the same procedure as the deacon. If a lay cantor sings the Exsultet, the celebrant does not impart his blessing. Moreover, the cantor does not incense the book or the candle, and the words in brackets "My dearest friends . . ." and "The Lord be with you" are omitted.[20] The "Amen" at the end of the Exsultet should be sung solemnly by all present.[21]

282.   At the end of the Exsultet, the deacon closes the book and returns to the chair. The thurifer returns to the sacristy. Incense will not be required again until the Gospel. All hand candles are now extinguished and set aside. A server takes the celebrant's candle to the credence table. If it is not already there, a server brings the Lectionary to the ambo and takes the book of the Exsultet to the credence table. All sit.

2. *Liturgy of the Word*

283.   The celebrant stands, and, attended by the book bearer, he introduces the readings, using or adapting the text provided or using his own words. There are seven Old Testament readings provided in the Lectionary, so that, together with the Epistle and Gospel, there are nine Scripture readings for the Vigil: "Wherever this is possible, all the readings should be read in order that the character of the Easter Vigil, which

---

these have been approved by the episcopal conference; cf. CLE, no. 84. But "alleluia" is not sung until the great Easter Alleluia before the Gospel.

[20] In this case the celebrant may incense the Easter candle immediately after he places it in the candlestick, just before the cantor goes to the ambo.

[21] In some places it is customary for the people to raise their hand candles while they sing this festive "Amen".

demands that it be somewhat prolonged, be respected at all costs."[22] However, for pastoral reasons, the seven Old Testament readings may be reduced to three. For the obvious reason of its paschal baptismal typology, the reading from Exodus 14 is never to be omitted.[23] The celebrant or a deacon may *briefly* introduce each reading.[24]

284. A designated responsorial psalm is sung by the choir, cantors and/or people after each reading.[25] The melodies chosen should promote the people's participation and devotion, but "[g]reat care is to be taken that trivial songs do not take the place of the psalms."[26] After the psalm, all stand as the celebrant sings or says the prayer, attended by the book bearer. He should pause for silent prayer after "let us pray". In some situations, the psalm may be replaced by a period of silent reflection, in which case there is no pause after "let us pray".[27] The lectors may be escorted to and from the ambo by the second M.C. or a server.

285. After the final reading and its prayer, the celebrant intones the Gloria. While the Gloria is being sung, the church bells and/or other bells are rung joyously.[28] Just before the Gloria begins, servers bring tapers from the credence table, light

---

[22] CLE, no. 85.

[23] Cf. MR, *Easter Vigil, Liturgy of the Word*, no. 21; CLE, no. 85.

[24] Cf. CLE, no. 86.

[25] It is useful to vary the style of music or the voices for each of the settings of these psalms or to use different instruments to accompany them, so as to avoid monotony.

[26] CLE, no. 86.

[27] Cf. MR, *Easter Vigil, Liturgy of the Word*, no. 23, a provision that would obviously apply where no choir or cantors were available.

[28] The bells may be pealed loudly only for a few moments before the Gloria is intoned, or they may be rung during the Gloria in a way that does not interfere with the singing, or, with due musical skill, they may even be rung as part of the setting of the Gloria.

them from the Easter candle, go to the main altar and light the six or four candles on or near it.[29] Then they light the candles at the twelve or four consecration crosses (if the church has been dedicated), the two processional candles on or near the credence table, and any other candles and lamps that have been prepared in the sanctuary or at side altars or shrines, but, at this stage, they do not light the lamp(s) before the tabernacle. The servers bring the tapers back to the credence table, extinguish them and then go to their places. This carefully planned procedure should be completed by the end of the Gloria.

286. Attended by the book bearer, the celebrant sings or says the Opening Prayer. Then all sit for the Epistle, Romans 6:3–11. After this reading, all stand, and, attended by the book bearer with the musical text, the celebrant intones the solemn Alleluia three times, raising the note a little higher each time.[30] Alternatively, the solemn Alleluia may be intoned by a cantor standing at a lectern or from the choir. The psalm is sung by cantor(s) or the choir, and all respond with "alleluia". Meanwhile, the thurifer approaches the chair, where, assisted by the deacon, the celebrant prepares incense as usual. The thurifer goes to a position so as to be able to lead the deacon to the ambo for the reading of the Gospel. The deacon seeks the celebrant's blessing. He goes to the altar, bows and takes up the Book of the Gospels. Only the thurifer leads the deacon (or a concelebrant or the celebrant) and the M.C. in the procession to the ambo, because, on this night, the Easter candle suffices to honor the risen Lord in his Gospel.[31] A homily is to be

---

[29] For the customary procedure, see CMRR, no. 859.

[30] Cf. CB, no. 352; CLE, no. 87.

[31] Cf. CB, no. 353. The two candle bearers, without candles, may escort the deacon in this procession, but this seems unnecessary.

given, no matter how brief,[32] and the content should take into account whether Baptism and Confirmation are about to be celebrated.

3. Liturgy of Baptism

287. There are three options for the Liturgy of Baptism: (a) Christian Initiation and the Blessing of the Font; (b) Blessing of the Font without Christian Initiation; (c) Blessing of Water. However, each option ends with the Renewal of Baptismal Promises.

OPTION (A): CHRISTIAN INITIATION AND THE BLESSING OF THE FONT

288. When possible the paschal sacraments of Christian Initiation should be celebrated during the Easter Vigil with the singing of the Litany and the solemn blessing of the font. This is the culmination of the Rite of Christian Initiation and thus should be regarded as the ideal form of celebrating the Vigil.

289. (i) When the sacraments are to be celebrated in a baptistery, the candidates for Baptism are first called forward. Attended by the book bearer carrying the Missal or order of Holy Week, the deacon or celebrant calls those to be baptized. With their sponsors, or brought by parents and godparents, and guided by the second M.C. or a server, they come forward and stand in front of the sanctuary, facing the altar. The celebrant asks the people for their prayers, using the instruction provided or his own words. The deacon (or, lacking a deacon, the first candle bearer) carefully takes the Easter candle from its stand. Together with the Missal or order of Holy Week, the book bearer takes up the

---

[32] Cf. CLE, no. 87.

appropriate volume of the Roman Ritual (unless this is already prepared on the table in the baptistery). Two cantor(s) begin to sing the Litany of the Saints, to which may be added the titular of the church, local patrons and the saints' names to be taken by those who will be baptized.

290. The procession goes to the baptistery in this order: the deacon (or first candle bearer) carrying the Easter candle, candidates and sponsors or infants with parents and godparents, second candle bearer and book bearer with the Missal (and Roman Ritual), the M.C., concelebrants, (a second deacon), the celebrant. The procession should move slowly, to keep pace with the singing of the Litany, and thus could take a longer route to the baptistery. The congregation should turn towards the baptistery for the celebration of the sacraments. On arrival at the baptistery, the M.C. ensures that the candidates and their sponsors, or the parents and godparents, are arranged so that they do not impede the view of the faithful.[33] The deacon may set the candle in a stand or bracket near the font or hand it to the first candle bearer. The second candle bearer stands near the table where the baptismal candles and white garments have been prepared.

291. (ii) However when the sacraments are celebrated at a font in or near the sanctuary, the deacon (or, lacking a deacon, the first candle bearer) carefully takes the Easter candle and leads the book bearer, second candle bearer, M.C., concelebrants and celebrant to the font or vessel of water. The candidates are called forward, the celebrant asks the people for their prayers, using the instruction provided or his own words, and *then* the Litany of the Saints is sung, all standing as is customary in the Easter Season.

---

[33] Cf. RCIA, no. 213.

292. (iii) At the conclusion of the Litany, attended by the book bearer with the Missal or order of Holy Week, the celebrant sings or says the Blessing of Water, hands joined. Just before "We ask you, Father . . .", the deacon or server may hand the celebrant the Easter candle, and, at these words, he may lower it once or three times into the water, holding the lower part of the candle immersed in the water until the end of the prayer.[34] As the choir and/or people sing the acclamation "Springs of water" or a similar baptismal acclamation, the celebrant slowly raises the candle from the baptismal water and gives it back to the deacon or server.[35]

293. (iv) The book bearer lays aside the Missal or order of Holy Week and takes up the Roman Ritual. He attends the celebrant as adult candidates for Baptism individually renounce the devil, profess their faith and are baptized by effusion or immersion. After Baptism, the second candle bearer gives the white garments to the sponsors. The celebrant says "N. and N., you have become . . ."; the sponsors put the white garments on the neophytes at the words "Take this white garment"; and the neophytes reply "Amen" at the end of the formula. The second candle bearer then gives each sponsor a baptismal candle. The celebrant touches the Easter candle, held by the deacon or server, and calls the sponsors forward. They light the baptismal candles from the Easter candle and give them to the neophytes. Then the celebrant says, "You have been enlightened . . . heavenly kingdom" and the neophytes reply "Amen".

294. (v) *Confirmation.* When the bishop baptizes adults, he always confirms them immediately after Baptism. All priests

---

[34] This sign of dying and rising again is optional but should always be included in the rite.

[35] Before Baptism by immersion, the M.C. ensures that some water is transferred into a large vessel for use during the Easter Season.

who baptize adults have the faculty to administer Confirmation, so, in normal circumstances, a priest celebrant will confirm those he has baptized at the Vigil.[36] Between the celebration of adult Baptism and Confirmation, an appropriate hymn, such as "You have put on Christ", may be sung.[37] If the Baptisms took place in the baptistery, Confirmation may be celebrated there, but it would seem preferable to return to the sanctuary for Confirmation. The bishop confirms in the sanctuary.[38] Therefore, during the hymn, the procession of the newly baptized, led once more by the deacon or server carrying the Easter candle, goes to the sanctuary for Confirmation. If the celebrant sits to confirm, servers may set up a faldstool or chair at the center of the sanctuary during the hymn. The deacon or server places the Easter candle in its stand, and the rite of Confirmation proceeds, beginning with the celebrant's address to the neophytes.[39] The book bearer attends the celebrant with the appropriate volume of the Roman Ritual or Roman Pontifical.

295.   The celebrant (rises if seated and) invites all present to pray for the outpouring of the Holy Spirit on the newly baptized. After a pause for silent prayer he extends his hands over the candidates for the prayer "All powerful God. . . ." If he chooses to confirm while seated, the M.C. or a server spreads a gremial veil (linen amice) over his knees as soon as he sits and ties it to the faldstool or chair. The deacon or, lacking a deacon, a concelebrant or the M.C. brings from the credence table the open vessel of Chrism, which the celebrant takes in his left hand. As each candidate kneels or

---

[36] Cf. CIC, Canon 883 §2. If Confirmation is not to be given to adults immediately after Baptism, the celebrant says the prayer and anoints each neophyte with Chrism in silence, as at the Baptism of Infants; cf. RCIA, no. 224.

[37] Cf. RCIA, no. 227; CB, no. 366.

[38] Cf. CB, no. 367.

[39] See RCIA, no. 229.

stands before him, the celebrant makes the sign of the cross with Chrism with his right thumb on the forehead while saying the sacramental form, "N. be sealed with the gift of the Holy Spirit." The newly confirmed responds "Amen." Then the celebrant says "Peace be with you", and the newly confirmed responds, "And also with you."[40]

296. Just before the anointing with Chrism, each sponsor should take the baptismal candle from the candidate and hold it in the left hand while placing the right hand on the neophyte's shoulder. The candidate or sponsor may quietly advise the celebrant of the candidate's Confirmation name, or the sponsor may hand a card bearing the name to the deacon, a concelebrant or the M.C., who stands next to the celebrant and advises him of the name just before the anointing. After the anointing, the sponsor gives the baptismal candle back to the newly confirmed, and, guided by the second M.C. or a server, they both return to their places in the baptistery, or at the front of the sanctuary, where they stand facing the altar. Then the Renewal of Baptismal Promises follows, as described below.

297. (vi) *Baptism of Infants*. After the blessing of baptismal water, the parents and godparents renounce the devil and profess the faith for them as usual. Baptism follows as set out in the rite for baptizing infants.[41] The newly baptized are anointed with Chrism, a white garment is put on each child, and then the second candle bearer gives the sponsors a baptismal candle which they light from the Easter candle. However the prayers of blessing the parents are omitted. The parents and godparents remain standing before the font or at the front

---

[40] Gently striking the left cheek during "Peace be with you" is no longer mentioned in the modern rite but may be maintained as a custom.

[41] See RR, *Rite of Baptism for Several Children*, nos. 55–60.

of the sanctuary, facing the altar, and the Renewal of Baptismal Promises follows, as described below.

OPTION (B): BLESSING OF THE FONT WITHOUT CHRISTIAN INITIATION

298. In a church where there is a font, but when the sacraments of Christian Initiation are not celebrated during the Easter Vigil, the Litany is sung and baptismal water is blessed for use during the Easter Season, as described above in option (a) iii, but omitting reference to candidates for Baptism in the rites and procession. Just before the Litany, or the blessing of the water, the celebrant uses a different call to prayer, provided in the Missal.[42] If this rite is celebrated in the baptistery, the procession may return to the sanctuary. Then the Renewal of Baptismal Promises follows, as described below.

OPTION (C): BLESSING OF WATER

299. In a church or chapel where there is no font, and when the sacraments of Christian Initiation are not celebrated during the Easter Vigil, the Litany and blessing of baptismal water are omitted and replaced by a simpler blessing of Easter water. The procession forms as described above and goes to the place where the vessel of water has been prepared, in or near the sanctuary. But the Easter candle is not taken from its stand and carried in procession because it will not be used for this form of the blessing of water. Alternatively, the procession may be omitted; the celebrant remains at the chair, and two servers bring the vessel of water before him. Standing before the vessel of water, attended by the book bearer with the Missal or order of Holy Week, the celebrant introduces the rite with the words provided or his

---

[42] Cf. MR, *Easter Vigil*, no. 40.

own words and then, with hands joined, he blesses the water by singing or saying the alternative prayer provided.[43] The Renewal of Baptismal Promises follows, as described in the following paragraph.

RENEWAL OF BAPTISMAL PROMISES

300. The second M.C. or a server ensures that everyone in the sanctuary (except the celebrant and book bearer) has a hand candle. Servers bring tapers from the credence table, light them from the Easter candle and move among the clergy and the faithful to ensure that all the hand candles are lit once more. At the same time, supervised by the M.C., the second candle bearer takes the jug, fills the holy water bucket with Easter water and gives it, with the sprinkler, to the deacon or, lacking a deacon, to the first candle bearer. Attended by the book bearer and standing near the font or large vessel of blessed water, or at the place where he administered Confirmation, the celebrant introduces the Renewal of Baptismal Promises with the words provided in the rite or his own words. After the rejection of Satan and Profession of Faith, he says the prayer, hands joined. Then, accompanied by the deacon(s) or first candle bearer and M.C., he passes through the church and sprinkles all present with Easter water, while the choir and/or people sing "Vidi aquam . . ." (I saw water) or some other appropriate baptismal antiphon or hymn.[44] All make the sign of the cross, as is customary when sprinkled with blessed water.

---

[43] Cf. MR, *Easter Vigil*, no. 54. It would seem appropriate to make the sign of the cross at "bless this water", even if this is not indicated in the text.

[44] Cf. MR, *Easter Vigil*, no. 56; CLE, no. 89. The singing should be prolonged, or solemn music may follow, to accompany the procession from the baptistery or the return to the chair from wherever water was blessed.

301. During the sprinkling, the sacristan(s) or server(s) take(s) the jug(s) of blessed water from the font or the large vessel and go(es) to the stoups at the various church doors and fill(s) each of them with water. Any water remaining is poured back into the font or large vessel, and the empty jugs are left there. When the celebrant returns to the sanctuary he lays aside the holy water bucket and sprinkler (which a server takes to the credence table); then he bows to the altar and goes to the chair. Guided by the second M.C. or a server, the neophytes and their sponsors, parents, godparents and newly baptized infants return to their designated places in the church.

302. However, if all these rites were celebrated in the baptistery, once the celebrant returns there, the procession forms as before, led by the deacon or server carrying the Easter candle, and goes to the sanctuary. The deacon or server sets the Easter candle in its stand. The neophytes and their sponsors, parents, godparents and newly baptized infants are guided back to their designated places by the second M.C. or a server. The celebrant and servers bow to the altar, and the celebrant goes to the chair.

303. If the baptismal water was not blessed at the font, the celebrant and servers come to the center of the sanctuary and bow to the altar, and the celebrant goes to the chair. The deacon or server sets the Easter candle in its stand. Directed by the M.C., the deacon and/or servers now take the large vessel of water to the font. However, if water was blessed in a church without a font, the large vessel is taken to some convenient place.[45]

---

[45] Cf. MR, *Easter Vigil*, no. 57. The "convenient place" would be accessible to the faithful who wish to take blessed water home with them after the Vigil.

Conclusion of the Liturgy of the Word

304. All the hand candles and baptismal candles are extinguished, and a server takes those of the clergy and other servers to the credence table. Having set the Easter candle in its stand, unless he is to read the intentions of the General Intercessions from the ambo, the deacon joins the celebrant at the chair. The book bearer takes the volume of the Ritual to the credence table and takes up the book for the General Intercessions and goes to wait near the chair.

305. At the chair, attended by the book bearer, the celebrant presides over the General Intercessions as usual. Escorted by the second M.C. or a server, the newly baptized adults take part in the Intercessions.[46] If there have been no baptisms, the deacon or lectors read the intentions. The Creed is omitted because the Profession of Faith has already been made in the Renewal of Baptismal Promises. The celebrant sits while the deacon(s), candle bearers and other servers bring the Missal, corporal and sacred vessels to the altar.

4. Liturgy of the Eucharist

306. The fourth stage and high point of the Vigil is the celebration of the Eucharistic Sacrifice. In the fullest sense this is *the* Easter sacrament, celebrating the Paschal Mystery and completing Christian Initiation. Therefore the Mass should be celebrated, not only with full solemnity and festive ceremonial, but without haste.[47]

307. Newly baptized adults and children, or the families of newly baptized infants, should take part in the procession of gifts.

---

[46] Cf. MR, *Easter Vigil*, no. 49.
[47] Cf. CLE, nos. 90–91.

Therefore, the second M.C. or a server leads them to the table of the gifts, gives them the vessels containing bread and wine. During a hymn, motet or other music, he leads them in procession to the sanctuary, once the altar has been prepared and the celebrant has gone to the center to receive the gifts. It is preferred that the Eucharistic Prayer be sung, that is, not only the Preface but the whole text.[48] In the First Preface of Easter, reference is made to "this night". When the First Eucharistic Prayer is chosen, the variations at "In union with the whole Church . . ." and "Father, accept this offering . . ." are used. Similar intercessions for the baptized and their godparents are provided for all the Eucharistic Prayers.

308. Communion under both species is commended at the Vigil Mass.[49] Newly baptized adults receive the Eucharist under both species. Moreover, if adults have been baptized and confirmed, before he says "This is the Lamb of God . . .", the celebrant may *briefly* address them on the excellence of the Eucharistic Mystery, which completes their initiation into the Body of Christ.[50] During or after Communion it is appropriate to sing Psalm 117 with the antiphon "Pascha nostrum", or Psalm 33 with the triple alleluia for an antiphon, or some other song of Easter joy.[51] Immediately after Communion, accompanied by a server with a lighted taper, the deacon (or lacking a deacon, the celebrant), or a concelebrant or an extraordinary minister, takes the Blessed Sacrament in a ciborium or ciboria to the tabernacle. Because eucharistic reservation has commenced once more, the veil is arranged over the tabernacle, according to custom,

---

[48] Cf. CLE, no. 91.
[49] Cf. CLE, no. 92, subject to the approval of the diocesan bishop.
[50] Cf. CB, no. 370.
[51] Cf. CLE, no. 91.

and the server lights the lamp(s) near the tabernacle. They both genuflect and return to their places in the sanctuary.

309. After the solemn Easter blessing,[52] the deacon (or, lacking a deacon, the celebrant) adds a double "alleluia" when he sings the dismissal, and all respond "Thanks be to God, alleluia, alleluia." The cross and processional candles are carried by their respective bearers in the final procession to the sacristy or vesting room. This procession should be accompanied by a triumphant hymn or appropriate joyous music.

310. After the Vigil, the Blessed Sacrament is brought from the "other place of reservation" and reposed in the tabernacle. The Easter candle is extinguished, preferably once the faithful have left the church. Servers should bring an adequate supply of baptismal water from the font or large vessel to the sacristy, where the sacristan sets it aside for use during the Easter Season. The large vessel of baptismal water may be left in the baptistery, in the sanctuary or some other place, so that the faithful may take the blessed water home after the Vigil.[53] In some places, the faithful also take the new fire home to light their own lamps or a family "Easter candle" for the paschal celebrations in the domestic church.

---

[52] The blessing at the conclusion of the *Rite of Baptism for Children* (nos. 70, 247–49) may be used when infants have been baptized at the Vigil; cf. CB, no. 370.

[53] It may be prudent to make available the blessed water only during times of worship, to avoid desecration or superstitious use. In some parishes it is put in small bottles and distributed widely throughout the whole community with advice as to its use. The sacramental thus becomes a way of re-evangelizing families.

The Bishop Presides at the Easter Vigil

311. All the variations that apply when a bishop is the celebrant of the Vigil rites are indicated in the *Ceremonial of Bishops*, nos. 332–70. He wears the ornate miter and carries the crozier. In the procession into the church with the Easter candle, the crozier bearer, carrying the crozier turned inwards, precedes the bishop. The bishop holds a lighted candle during the singing of the Exsultet. Then he sits, wearing the miter, and introduces the readings.[54] It should also be noted that, after the reading of the Epistle, a deacon or lector may, and should, go to the bishop at the cathedra or chair to introduce the solemn Alleluia. He bows to the bishop and says, "Most Reverend Father, I bring you a message of great joy, the message of Alleluia." Then, the miter is removed, all stand and the bishop intones the paschal Alleluia.[55]

On the third day the friends of Christ coming at daybreak to the place found the grave empty and the stone rolled away. In varying ways they realised the new wonder; but even they hardly realised that the world had died in the night. What they were looking at was the first day of a new creation, with a new heaven and a new earth; and in the semblance of the gardener God walked again in the garden, in the cool not of the evening but the dawn.

— G. K. Chesterton, *The Everlasting Man*

---

[54] Cf. CB, no. 346, which adds that he may assign the introduction to the readings to a deacon or concelebrant.

[55] Cf. CB, no. 352. When intoning on the three rising notes he may be assisted by a deacon or concelebrant.

10.

Easter and Pentecost

312. The Christian year reaches its supreme moments in the celebration of the Lord Jesus Christ, the Incarnate Word, risen indeed in our human flesh, glorified in that flesh, triumphant over the mortality of that flesh. Again and again, the liturgy resounds with the cry of "alleluia!", as the people reborn through the Paschal Mystery wait in joyful hope for the day when they too will share the glory of their risen Lord. From Easter morning through Pentecost, the Regina Cæli replaces the Angelus. The Liturgy of the Hours contains an abundance of "alleluias" during these weeks.

313. Easter is the "Feast of feasts", the "Solemnity of solemnities" and the "Great Sunday".[1] Festive solemnity should mark all the Masses celebrated on Easter Sunday, the supreme day of the Christian year.[2] One of the Easter Masses, in addition to the Vigil, should be solemnly sung. In some places it is customary to precede this Mass with a procession, that is, a form of solemn entrance.[3] The Easter candle is lit for all Masses; its candlestick is placed to one side of the ambo or near the altar.[4] A vessel containing blessed Easter

---

[1] Cf. CCC, no. 1169, citing Saint Athanasius, *Ep. fest*, 1.

[2] Cf. CLE, no. 97.

[3] A robed choir could take part in this procession, and, according to local custom, banners could be carried by servers or members of lay sodalities.

[4] In some countries, a figure of the risen Christ is set up in the sanctuary. While such a custom should be respected, the Easter candle remains the liturgical sign of the risen Lord and should predominate.

water and a sprinkler are prepared on the credence table for the sprinkling of Easter water, either in place of the Penitential Rite (with the singing of "Vidi aquam") or at the Renewal of Baptismal Promises, which preferably should replace the Creed at all Masses. If they have not already been filled during the Vigil, the stoups at the church doors are replenished with Easter water.[5]

314. The Easter Sequence, "Victimæ Paschali", should be sung or at least recited before the Gospel at all Masses. The homily may well be a joyous proclamation of the historical event of the Lord's Resurrection, its salvific meaning in our lives today and our hope of resurrection in Christ.[6]

The Renewal of Baptismal Promises

315. After the homily the celebrant stands at the chair, or in front of the altar, attended by the book bearer with the Missal. The deacon, M.C. or a server stands on his right carrying the vessel of blessed Easter water and sprinkler. The celebrant may use his own words to introduce the rite. After the final question of the Profession of Faith, he takes the sprinkler and, accompanied by the deacon, M.C. or server, goes among the people sprinkling them. All make the sign of the cross as they are sprinkled. An appropriate antiphon such as "Vidi aquam", a psalm or short hymn on the theme of Baptism and the Resurrection is sung. He pauses in front of the altar and hands the sprinkler (and vessel) to the deacon or server; all bow or genuflect, and he returns to the chair for the General Intercessions.

316. In the First Preface of Easter, reference is made to "this Easter day". When the First Eucharistic Prayer is chosen,

---

[5] Cf. CLE, no. 97.
[6] Cf. CCC, nos. 272, 638–55, 988–1004.

the variations at "In union with the whole Church . . ." and
"Father, accept this offering . . ." are used. Variations indicated in the other Eucharistic Prayers are to be used. The
deacon or celebrant adds a double "alleluia" to the dismissal
at Mass and the major Hours, and all respond "Thanks be
to God, alleluia, alleluia."[7]

317. On the night of Easter Sunday, where customary, psalms
should be sung during a procession to the baptismal font.[8]
This is the tradition of "baptismal Vespers", a celebration for the newly baptized, leading into the postbaptismal
catechesis or mystagogy with which the Christian community accompanies them especially during the Easter Oc
tave and throughout the Easter Season. Throughout these
weeks, special places in the church may be allocated to the
neophytes and their godparents, if this is thought to be
pastorally prudent. They should also be included in the
General Intercessions.[9]

The Easter Octave

318. All the variations for Mass on Easter Sunday apply during
celebrations of Mass and the Liturgy of the Hours for the
whole of the *Easter Octave*, that is, the week up to and including the Second Sunday of Easter. This Sunday, "Do-
minica in albis", was formerly known as "Low Sunday".
It is now also designated as Divine Mercy Sunday.[10] The
Easter Sequence, "Victimæ Paschali", should be sung or at
least recited before the Gospel at all Masses. The Gloria is

---

[7] During Benediction, where the versicle "Panem de cælo" is still customarily
sung, "alleluia" is added once after the versicle and its response.

[8] Cf. CB, no. 371; CLE, no. 98.

[9] Cf. CLE, no. 103.

[10] For this option, see below, chapter 11, no. 385.

said or sung at the weekday Masses during the octave, but the Creed is omitted. The Easter Sunday psalms and their antiphons are used at Lauds and Vespers on all the days of the octave, but proper psalms are assigned for the other hours for each day. At Lauds, Vespers and Compline, the responsory is replaced by "This is the day . . .". The Easter candle should be lit at all public celebrations of Mass, the sacraments and the Liturgy of the Hours during the octave. The Eucharist should be brought to the sick during the Easter Octave, so that they may be associated with the Paschal celebration of the whole Church.[11]

Easter Season

319. The "Great Sunday" of the fifty days of the Easter Season recalls the time when the risen Lord manifested himself to his disciples, culminating in his Ascension and the outpouring of the Holy Spirit on the apostles at Pentecost. Sundays in this season have precedence over all feasts of the Lord and solemnities. If a solemnity falls on a Sunday in Easter Season, it is anticipated on the Saturday. Nor are weekday celebrations in honor of Our Lady or the saints permitted to be transferred to these Sundays.[12] Throughout this time, the postbaptismal catechesis of the newly baptized is focused on homilies based especially on the Sunday readings for cycle A.[13] The First Communion of children may well be celebrated on a Sunday in Easter Season.[14] The faithful should also be instructed about the "Easter precept" to

---

[11] "Highly recommended" in CLE, no. 104.

[12] Cf. LY, nos. 5, 23 and 58.

[13] See, CB, no. 374, citing RCIA, no. 237 (U.S. edition, no. 247).

[14] Cf. CLE, no. 103.

receive the Eucharist during this time, as defined by the episcopal conference.[15]

320. On the Sundays in the Easter Season, the sprinkling with holy water at the beginning of Mass is accompanied by the singing of "Vidi aquam . . ." (I saw water) or a similar antiphon or hymn. The Fourth Sunday of Easter, "Good Shepherd Sunday", is the world day set aside by the Holy Father for prayers for priestly and religious vocations. The homily and the General Intercessions should develop this theme.[16] Throughout the Easter Season the Easter water is used for all Baptisms. The Easter candle is lit at least during all the more solemn celebrations of the season up to and including Pentecost Sunday.[17]

321. In some communities it is customary for houses to be blessed to celebrate the Lord's Resurrection. After the Solemnity of Easter and never before it, this blessing is given by the parish priest, or other priests or deacons delegated by him. The rite is found in the *Book of Blessings*. In a city where there are many apartments or houses to visit, several families may gather for a common celebration of the blessing.[18] This is an excellent opportunity for pastoral visitation. It might well be combined with Communion for the sick and elderly.

---

[15] Cf. CIC, Canon 920.
[16] See CCC, nos. 874–79, 1536–1600, on the priesthood; 914–33, on the religious life.
[17] Cf. CLE, no. 99.
[18] Cf. CLE, no. 105.

The Ascension of the Lord

322. The visible manifestations of the risen Lord Jesus terminated in a definitive moment of mission, farewell and departure, which took the form of his glorious Ascension into heaven in the sight of the apostles. In this event we encounter the fascinating challenge of Christian eschatology, the tension between "now" and "not yet". He who departs is still with us. He who ascends is our High Priest, interceding for us before the Father. He who goes up in glory will return again to judge the living and the dead, for this is a celebration of his eternal Kingship.

323. The Solemnity of the Ascension is celebrated either on the Thursday after the Sixth Sunday of Easter or, according to the decision of the episcopal conference, on the Seventh Sunday of Easter. When the Ascension is celebrated on the Sunday, the Missal and Lectionary provide propers for the Thursday after the Sixth Sunday of Easter. The third edition of the Roman Missal provides a proper Mass for the Vigil of the Ascension and restores the collect of the 1962 missal as an option for the Mass of the day. The homily on the Ascension may well develop the themes of Christ ever interceding for us as our great High Priest in heaven, his abiding presence in the Church "until the consummation of the ages", his future return in glory and his Kingship.[19] When the First Eucharistic Prayer is chosen, the variation at "In union with the whole Church . . ." is used. The Easter candle is lit at all Masses and is not extinguished after the Gospel.

---

[19] Cf. CCC, nos. 659–82.

Pentecost Sunday

324. As the Lord Jesus promised, the Holy Spirit is poured out upon the Church, gathered in prayer in the upper room around Mary. The signs of wind and fire, the gifts of courage, eloquence and languages envelop and empower those chosen to be the beginning of the Church. Born from the pierced side of Christ, washed in his blood and nourished by his flesh, they are espoused to him forever. Now, as witnesses to his Resurrection, they go forth on his saving mission that transforms the world. Through the power of the Holy Spirit they will form a new humanity, the living Body of Christ where all will be one in the Paraclete poured out at Pentecost.

325. After Easter, the Solemnity of Pentecost is the second most important day in the Church year. Pentecost concludes the Easter Season, therefore the bishop should celebrate a stational Mass and preside over the Liturgy of the Hours.[20] The Vigil Mass of Pentecost should be marked by solemnity and may be the culmination of a longer vigil of prayer and readings. Unlike the Easter Vigil, this celebration is not baptismal, rather an attentive watching in "urgent prayer", following the example of Our Lady and the apostles and disciples awaiting the coming of the Holy Spirit.[21] The liturgical color is red.

326. The principal Mass of the day should be celebrated with greater solemnity. At all Masses, the Pentecost Sequence, "Veni Sancte Spiritus", should be sung or at least recited before the Gospel. When the First Eucharistic Prayer is chosen, the variation at "In union with the whole Church . . ."

[20] Cf. CB, no. 376.
[21] Cf. CLE, no. 107.

is used. The homily may well develop the meaning of the transforming, strengthening and healing power of the Holy Spirit in the lives of the apostles, hence in our lives today.[22] Because the Solemnity of Pentecost marks the end of the "Great Sunday" of the Easter Season, the deacon or celebrant adds a double "alleluia" to the dismissal at Mass and the major Hours, and all respond "Thanks be to God, alleluia, alleluia."

327. In some places, the Sacrament of Confirmation is celebrated on Pentecost Sunday, but the proper texts of the Mass of the day are to be used. Red vestments are worn for all Masses. On or about Pentecost Sunday, a special celebration should be held to conclude the mystagogical catechesis of the newly baptized.[23] This might well be linked to the last Mass of Pentecost, which could be combined with Second Vespers of the solemnity. However, such a celebration should not be linked to a Pentecost vigil, whose character, as noted, is not baptismal.

328. At the conclusion of the last Mass of Pentecost,[24] the Easter candle is taken to the baptistery and set up near the font in its candlestick or bracket. It would seem appropriate to transfer the burning candle in procession, during the recessional hymn or an appropriate antiphon or motet. The transfer of the candle may well be carried out in the following way. After the dismissal, incense is prepared and blessed. Then the deacon (or, lacking a deacon, the celebrant) takes the

---

[22] Cf. CCC, nos. 683–741; the Church as the temple of the Spirit, nos. 797–99; her holiness, nos. 823–28; the Sacrament of Confirmation, nos. 1285–321; gifts and fruits of the Spirit, nos. 1830–32; prayer in the Spirit, nos. 2670–72.

[23] Cf. CLE, no. 103. This celebration may take place on the Solemnity of the Ascension.

[24] Or Second Vespers of Pentecost, where this is the final liturgical celebration of the day.

Easter candle, and, preceded by the thurifer, cross bearer and candle bearers (preferably without candles), he carries it to the baptistery, where it is placed in its candlestick or bracket. The celebrant may incense it with three double swings; then the procession returns to the sacristy or vesting room as usual. The candle should be extinguished after the people have left the church.

329. After Pentecost, the Easter candle is used for the celebration of Baptisms and funeral rites. However, except when it is needed for these celebrations, it is never brought to the sanctuary and lit during Mass or other rites.[25] The Easter Season ends after Compline on Pentecost Sunday. The Season of the Year begins once more on the Monday after Pentecost, as will be explained below, no. 337.[26]

Prayer for Christian Unity

330. In some countries, the Octave of Prayer for Christian Unity commences on Ascension Thursday and concludes on Pentecost Sunday. A series of themes is usually approved by the Ordinary and episcopal conference or by an ecumenical body to promote prayers for specific intentions on each day of this non-liturgical octave. The Mass for Christian Unity should be celebrated when the day permits. Ecumenical forms of worship and meetings may appropriately include welcoming other Christians to take part in the festive celebration of the Liturgy of the Hours.

---

[25] Cf. CLE, no. 99. This restriction is meant to protect the specific paschal-baptismal symbolism of the Easter candle.

[26] In some places, the Monday and Tuesday after Pentecost are days of devotion to the Holy Spirit in light of the octave of the old calendar. A votive Mass of the Holy Spirit may be offered on these days.

Rogation and Ember Days

331. The Rogation or Ember days were traditionally observed on the Feast of Saint Mark, April 25, and on the Monday, Tuesday and Wednesday before the Ascension of Our Lord. On these days it was customary to pray for the needs of all people, and especially for the productivity of the earth and human labor, rendering thanks to our bountiful Lord for his goodness revealed in creation. The episcopal conference should reorder the celebration of these days to meet local conditions.[27] Obviously this intensive intercession and thanksgiving responds to times either of planting or harvest and vintage in the rural societies in both hemispheres. But the prayer may also be adapted in industrialized societies to render thanks to God for his bounty or to thank him for the nation or to celebrate human labor. The details of observing these days pertain to the Ordinary, who should ensure that the celebration includes an emphasis on the ministry of charity.[28]

332. A Mass for various needs and occasions that is appropriate to the local situation should be chosen.[29] In accord with our Roman tradition, a solemn procession with the singing of the Litany of the Saints takes place before this Mass. In times past, the rogations involved neighboring parishes, so that the procession moved from one church to another. The traditional color for the Litany procession is violet, but this

---

[27] Cf. CB, nos. 381–82. One obvious problem was the timing of these days in the former Roman Calendar. The days were tied to northern seasons, which made sense until the Southern Hemisphere was evangelized.

[28] Cf. CB, no. 383.

[29] Cf. CB, no. 384. Appropriate Masses in the MR: 21: For the nation; 29: For the progress of peoples; 26: For the blessing of man's labor; 27: For productive land; 28: After the harvest; 49: In thanksgiving.

would not seem appropriate if the designated Mass that follows were celebrated in white vestments or if the emphasis were to be on thanksgiving rather than intercession.

333. The traditional rogation procession takes place as follows. The procession first forms in front of the altar, with the cross and candle bearers to the left side, facing across. The celebrant, deacon(s) and other clergy and servers face the altar. All kneel in silent prayer; then a prescribed antiphon is sung, followed by the Litany.[30] All rise after "Holy Mary, Mother of God, pray for us", and the procession begins.

334. The cross and candle bearers lead the procession, but incense is not used. The cantors and/or choir follow the cross, then other servers, clergy in choir dress, the M.C., concelebrants, deacon(s), wearing the dalmatic, and the celebrant, wearing a cope. The faithful follow the celebrant. They should have the text of the litanies and any other prescribed prayers to ensure active participation. If the procession is long, the litany may be repeated, and penitential psalms or approved antiphons and hymns may be sung.

335. On returning to the church, or on arriving at another church where the Mass will be celebrated, the procession goes to the sanctuary and is formed in the same way as before the procession. If prescribed, the final prayers are sung or said; then incense is prepared, and the Mass begins as usual with the incensation of the altar while an entrance hymn or antiphon is sung. At the chair, the celebrant's cope is replaced with a chasuble. The Mass begins with the Opening Prayer or Gloria, and the Penitential Rite is omitted.[31] The homily will develop the theme of intercession or thanksgiving for

---

[30] The traditional rite is found in the former RR, X, iv.

[31] This is by analogy to the procedure followed after the processions for the Presentation of the Lord and Palm Sunday.

the bounty of God revealed in the wisdom and splendor of his creation.

> All time is God's time. On the other hand . . . the time of the Church is a "between" time, between the shadow and the reality, and so its special structure demands a sign, a time specially chosen and designated to draw time as a whole into the hands of God.
>
> —Joseph Cardinal Ratzinger, *The Spirit of the Liturgy*

II.

The Season of the Year

336. The year of the Church settles into the time of growth, the Season of the Year, sometimes called "Ordinary Time".[1] But this longest phase of the year of grace is in no sense "ordinary". The dignity of Sunday, insisted on by the Fathers of the Second Vatican Council,[2] is meant to shine forth, prolonging the joy of Easter and Pentecost, to celebrate the whole mystery of Christ.

337. The Season of the Year in fact begins on the Monday following January 6 (or Epiphany Sunday) and commences once more on the Monday after Pentecost. Distinctive features of the Easter Season cease. The first weeks of the major phase of the Season of the Year are marked by two solemnities, Trinity Sunday and Corpus Christi, and the longest season of the liturgical year concludes with the celebration of the Solemnity of Christ the King on the Thirty-Fourth Sunday.

338. In the Season of the Year the liturgical color is green on Sundays and ferial days. "Asperges me . . ." or another antiphon replaces "Vidi aquam . . ." at the blessing and sprinkling of holy water. The "alleluia" is no longer added to the introit and Communion verse, or to most antiphons and responsories, but it is retained for the verse sung before the Gospel and at the end of the versicles at the beginning of the

---

[1] The unfortunate expression "Ordinary Time" has been replaced by the Season of the Year.

[2] Cf. SC, no. 106, and see CCC, nos. 1166–67.

Liturgy of the Hours. The other Marian antiphons replace Regina Cæli after Compline. At morning, noon and dusk, beginning on the Monday after Pentecost, the Angelus replaces the Regina Cæli.

Trinity Sunday

339. The Mystery of the triune God is appropriately celebrated as a solemnity on the Sunday after Pentecost. We worship the Holy Trinity, and we worship in and through the Trinity. Every Eucharistic Celebration thus begins "In the name of the Father and of the Son and of the Holy Spirit" and concludes with the blessing given in the name of the Trinity. The high point of the Mass, the Eucharistic Prayer, is trinitarian in its structure, as expressed in the Ter Sanctus and the final doxology, "Per ipsum. . . ." The Mass itself, as the great memorial of the Cross and Easter, draws us into the Trinity and reveals the self-giving Love of the three Divine Persons who are One.[3]

340. The principal Mass of the day should be celebrated solemnly. The homilist's duty of preaching on the Holy Trinity may be made easier by presenting the trinitarian movement of the liturgy; for example, he might explain the final doxology of the Eucharistic Prayer or the way the Mass begins and concludes with the invocation of the Trinity, not forgetting the great acclamation during the Eucharistic Prayer, the Sanctus. The vestments are white. In some dioceses, and customarily in Rome, Holy Orders are conferred on Trinity Sunday, but the Mass of the solemnity is used, with the proper readings and white vestments.

---

[3] Cf. CCC, nos. 232–67.

Corpus Christi

341. The Solemnity of the Body and Blood of the Lord, known as Corpus Christi or Corpus Domini, is celebrated on the Thursday after Trinity Sunday or, according to the decision of the episcopal conference, on the following Sunday. The liturgical color is white. The sequence "Lauda Sion . . ." should be sung, or at least recited, before the Gospel. The eucharistic doctrine in the homily should reflect each of the distinct emphases in the three-year cycle of readings: A: the real presence of Jesus Christ in the Holy Eucharist; B: the Sacrifice of the New Covenant; C: Christ nourishing his Church in the Eucharist.

342. On this solemnity it is customary to honor our eucharistic Lord not only with a solemn Mass but with a procession of the Blessed Sacrament. This is described in detail in *Ceremonies of the Modern Roman Rite*, nos. 695–711.[4] The procession normally commences immediately after the principal Mass, so that a Host consecrated during this celebration may be carried in procession, but it may also be deferred until after a prolonged period of adoration.[5] The diocesan bishop regulates the procession. In some societies, he will judge that it is more prudent to hold the procession on Catholic property rather than taking it through the streets. However, there is no need to be too sensitive about risks of profanation, which can be avoided if the procession is well-organized and protected by the civil authorities. There is much to be said for the evangelizing power of a reverent act of witness to the Real Presence of Jesus Christ. Nor should

---

[4] The Blessed Sacrament, clergy and servers always come *first* in this procession. See appendix 10, diagram, p. 225.

[5] Cf. CB, no. 387.

Christians readily give in to pressure from those secularists who wish to banish all public manifestations of religion.

343. When it is not possible to hold a procession, the day should always include time for solemn exposition and public adoration of the Blessed Sacrament, concluded by Benediction. The Blessed Sacrament could be exposed after Communion at the final Mass of the morning.[6] Exposition and silent adoration would then continue during the afternoon, concluded by eucharistic devotions and Benediction, either celebrated before an evening Mass or combined with the Second Vespers of the solemnity. The sanctuary and altar of exposition should be adorned with distinctive splendor on this day of solemn eucharistic adoration.[7]

Sundays in the Season of the Year

344. The Second Vatican Council furthered the recovery of the place of honor for Sundays that began with the reforms of Pope Saint Pius X. The Council Fathers taught that the Lord's day is the original feast day. Believers should be helped to see it as a day of joy and freedom. Other celebrations shall not take precedence over this day, for Sunday is the foundation and the nucleus of the entire liturgical year.[8] In his Apostolic Letter *Dies Domini*, Pope John Paul II focused on the role of Sunday as the day of the risen Lord and of the gift of the Spirit, the true weekly Easter.[9] Moreover, "through sharing in the Eucharist, *the Lord's Day*

---

[6] Sacristans may reverently arrange extra flowers and lights on the altar or in the sanctuary immediately after Mass, that is, after exposition has begun.

[7] See CMRR, no. 668, and its footnotes 6 and 7.

[8] Cf. *Sacrosanctum Concilium* (hereafter SC), no. 106.

[9] Cf. John Paul II, Apostolic Letter *Dies Domini* (May 31, 1998), 19.

also becomes *the day of the Church*, when she can effectively exercise her role as the sacrament of unity."[10]

345. The tradition remains unchanged that in each parish on every Sunday the main act of worship should be a "High Mass" with music and full ceremonial. The solemn rite is the normal form of celebrating the liturgy according to the Roman Rite. Unfortunately, in spite of the flexible levels of solemnity offered in the postconciliar liturgy, the former practice of celebrating Sunday with only a series of "Low Masses" lingers in some parishes, under the guise of said Masses interspersed with a few hymns or religious songs. Nevertheless, with careful planning, one celebration of Mass every Sunday can easily be distinguished by a certain "exterior solemnity", even in a humble mission church. A choir, cantor and several lectors and servers can assist at this Mass. An M.C., perhaps a senior server, can direct the rite and the processional cross; processional candles and incense are used.

346. The Saturday night "vigil Mass" for Sunday has become popular. However, it should not be timed too early. The diocesan bishops should issue a directive to regulate when this Mass is to be celebrated. Confessions should be heard before and after, and even during, the Saturday evening Mass.[11]

347. Providing a certain variety among the Sunday Eucharistic Celebrations has been found pastorally useful in many parishes. The earlier Masses may take a relatively simple

---

[10] John Paul II, Apostolic Letter *Novo Millennio Ineunte: At the Beginning of the New Millennium* (January 6, 2001), 36.

[11] Should confessions be heard during Mass? In the author's opinion, yes. In this case pastoral need, the "good of souls", takes precedence over liturgical "correctness", at least on certain opportune occasions.

form, for those who seek a "quiet Mass", while a later Mass should include full ceremonial, music and singing. The pastor may also arrange for Sunday Masses to meet the needs of ethnic groups, young people, etc., but he should always be attentive lest "special" Masses divide the community. When choosing the time of these celebrations, he should also be careful not to impose on the wider parish community a form of liturgy that would be more appropriate for children or a youth group or the interests and spirituality of a particular religious movement or sodality.

Solemnities in the Season of the Year

348. On solemnities a priest is bound to follow the calendar of the church where he celebrates Mass.[12] As well as Trinity Sunday, Corpus Christi, All Saints and Christ the King, five other solemnities always fall within the Season of the Year.

349. *The Solemnity of the Sacred Heart* is celebrated on the Friday after the first Sunday after Trinity Sunday. In some places the charity of Christ is reflected in special collections of money, food and clothing for the poor, which may be incorporated in the procession of the gifts. The liturgical color is white.

350. *The Birthday of Saint John the Baptist* is celebrated on June 24. The great precursor of the Lord ranks at a high level in the liturgies of the West and the East. The liturgical color is white.

351. *The Solemnity of Saint Peter and Saint Paul* is celebrated on June 29. On this day there should be preaching on the pre-

---

[12] Cf. GIRM, no. 353.

rogatives of the Supreme Pontiff and the missionary dimension of the Church. The liturgical color is red.

352. *The Assumption of Our Lady* remains a holy day of obligation in most countries. Where this is not a public holiday, for pastoral reasons the major sung Masses should be the vigil Mass and an evening Mass. The liturgical color is white.

Notable Feasts and Memorials

353. Some days should be carefully noted in the course of the Season of the Year because they stand out or enjoy special liturgical privileges. They may include liturgical variants or are accompanied by popular devotions.

354. The Feast of the Visitation of Our Lady, May 31, is appropriately observed in some places as a celebration of the reality and sanctity of human life in the womb. The liturgical color is white.

355. The Memorial of the Immaculate Heart of Mary is celebrated on the day after the Solemnity of the Sacred Heart. This Saturday is now an obligatory memorial. The liturgical color is white.

356. The Memorial of Saint Anthony of Padua, June 13, is a day of special devotion to a popular saint in various ethnic communities. Customs such as the blessing of bread, children or flowers preferably take place after Mass and may be associated with a procession in honor of the saint. The liturgical color is white.

357. The Feast of the Transfiguration of the Lord, August 6, is a day of great importance in the Christian East and hence offers an occasion for prayer for Christian unity. In the

Roman Rite this event is also celebrated on the Second Sunday of Lent when the Gospel is one of the three accounts of the Transfiguration. The liturgical color is white.

358. The Feast of the Birth of the Blessed Virgin Mary, September 8, is a popular celebration of the Blessed Mother. By growing custom the Rosary is often recited in public on this day as a gift to honor Mary on her birthday. The liturgical color is white.

359. The Memorial of Our Lady of Sorrows, September 15, is marked by the traditional sequence "Stabat Mater", which should be sung or said before the Gospel, as indicated in the Lectionary. The liturgical color is white.

360. The Feast of Saints Michael, Gabriel and Raphael, Archangels, September 29, and the Memorial of the Guardian Angels, October 2, should be publicized and observed with some exterior solemnity to affirm the reality of the holy angels and their relationship to us in the divine plan of salvation. The liturgical color is white.

361. The Memorial of Saint Thérèse of the Child Jesus, Doctor of the Church, October 1, is a day of popular devotion. In some places the Carmelite custom of blessing roses is observed. This is an appropriate occasion for a youth pilgrimage. The liturgical color is white.

362. In some places the Memorial of Saint Francis of Assisi, October 4, includes the custom of blessing animals. The liturgical color is white.

National Celebrations

363. Solemnities, feasts and memorials that are specific to national calendars are indicated in appendix 8, "National

Celebrations". It should be noted that December 12 has been designated as the Feast of Our Lady of Guadalupe, patroness of the Americas; hence it is to be observed throughout the whole continent. Because the image revealed to Saint Juan Diego is believed to depict Mary Immaculate during her pregnancy, the feast may well include some emphasis on the unborn and their mothers. The liturgical color is white.

Celebration of Ecclesial Anniversaries

364. The following days are usually included in the Ordo for the nation or diocese and should be celebrated in a distinct way. Bringing these anniversaries to the attention of the faithful strengthens their attachment to the Universal Church and the particular Church. When they happen to coincide with a solemnity, these days are not observed or, in some instances, may be translated to another day. The phrase "all churches in the diocese" encompasses not only parish churches but all other churches, chapels and oratories, including those of exempt religious.

365. 1. *The anniversary of the election or installation of the Supreme Pontiff* is observed with Mass for the Pope and his intentions. It is also customary in some places to offer Mass for the Pope on his "onomastico" (the celebration of the saint of his baptismal name).

366. 2. *The anniversary of the death of the previous Pope* should be observed with a Requiem Mass in the cathedral and all other churches. On this day, it may be customary to set up a portrait of the deceased Pope near the sanctuary.

367. 3. *The anniversary of the episcopal ordination of the diocesan bishop* should be observed in a suitable way in the cathedral

and all churches of the diocese.[13] If the day permits, the Mass for the Church or for the bishop is celebrated, as provided in the Roman Missal, Masses for Various Needs and Occasions. The name of the bishop should also be included in the General Intercessions on this day.

368. 4. In the cathedral, *Requiem Mass* should be celebrated for the deceased predecessor of the diocesan bishop, unless he had been transferred to another diocese.[14] Likewise, Mass should be celebrated in the cathedral for all the deceased bishops of the diocese, either on each of their anniversaries or together on some specific day, for example during November.

369. 5. *The patron saint of the diocese* is celebrated as a feast in all churches within the diocese. For pastoral reasons, especially when the saint has some historical connection with the diocese, the bishop may direct that this day be observed as a solemnity.

370. 6. *The anniversary of the dedication of the cathedral* is celebrated as a solemnity in the cathedral and as a feast in all other churches of the diocese. The liturgical color is white, and the Mass is taken from the Common of the Dedication of a Church, with a Gloria and three readings. The Creed is said in the cathedral as befits a solemnity. The Liturgy of the Hours is taken from the Common of the Dedication of a Church with the adaptations that depend on whether the office is celebrated in the cathedral or other churches.

371. 7. *The anniversary of the dedication of a church* is observed as a solemnity in that building. A more solemn form of sung

---

[13] Cf. CB, no. 1167.
[14] Cf. CB, no. 1168.

Mass should be celebrated at a convenient time. Candles burn on the brackets set before the twelve or four consecration crosses, at least during all Masses and public celebrations of the Liturgy of the Hours. The liturgical color is white, and the Mass is taken from the Common of the Dedication of a Church, with the Gloria, three readings and the Creed. The Liturgy of the Hours is taken from the Common of the Dedication of a Church following the variations provided when the office is celebrated in the church of dedication.

372. 8. *The feast of the title of a church* is observed as a solemnity. A more solemn form of sung Mass should be celebrated at a convenient time. In practice, the way this day is observed varies according to local customs, the popularity of the saint or whether the title of the church is that of a Christian mystery rather than a saint.

Weekday Mass

373. Although it usually takes a simpler form in terms of ceremonial, the weekday Mass should reflect the diversity of liturgical ministries associated with Sunday celebrations of the Eucharist. The celebrant should be assisted by a lector and a server. Permanent or transitory deacons resident in the parish or religious community should also fulfill their ministry at weekday Masses. Acolytes and other authorized extraordinary ministers of the Eucharist may be invited to help, but only according to need, for example where Communion is given in both kinds.

374. A brief homily on the readings or the saint of the day and a *short* set of General Intercessions should be a normal part of the weekday rite. Care should be taken to avoid always

using the Second Eucharistic Prayer.[15] The pastor will also discern the possibilities of the people singing parts of the Mass or hymns, at least at some weekday Masses. In many urban or suburban parishes a midmorning Mass has become popular, with senior citizens and mothers attending in significant numbers. Because there is more time for this celebration than for an earlier Mass for commuters, the liturgy can be developed in terms of preaching and music. The timing of this liturgy also provides another opportunity when confessions can be heard before or after Mass. In the rural situation, the pastor discerns the timing of the daily celebration of the Eucharist in the light of the working pattern of farming people's lives, which varies not only from place to place but according to the natural seasons.

Choosing an Appropriate Weekday Mass

375. On weekdays the celebrant is to observe the feasts and obligatory memorials set out in the calendar of the church where he celebrates a public Mass.[16] On feasts he may celebrate a Ritual Mass for a sacrament, such as Baptism or Marriage, and the funeral Mass, but he may not celebrate a Mass for various needs and occasions or Mass on the occasion of news of a death, final burial or first anniversary. On optional memorials, however, he is free to celebrate not only a Ritual Mass and the funeral Mass, but also a Mass for various needs and occasions (if there is a good pastoral reason) and Requiem Mass on the occasion of news of a death, final burial or first anniversary. All these Masses may be said on optional memorials and ferial days.

---

[15] When time is a problem, the length of the readings can be taken into account in deciding which Eucharistic Prayer is appropriate.

[16] Cf. GIRM, no. 354 a. But no. 354 b. allows him to follow "his own calendar" (e.g., of his Order) when celebrating Mass without a congregation.

376. When an optional memorial is indicated, he is free to choose it. However, on the privileged weekdays of Advent, that is, from December 17 to 24, on the days of the Christmas Octave and on the weekdays of Lent, only the Opening Prayer of an optional memorial is said. No memorials are observed on Ash Wednesday and the weekdays of Holy Week.[17] On the other weekdays of Advent, up to December 17 and the weekdays of the seasons of Christmas (from January 2) and Easter, he may choose the weekday Mass, an optional memorial, the Mass of a saint listed in the Martyrology for that day (but not found in the Ordo), or a Mass for some need or occasion.[18]

377. On ferial days in the Season of the Year the celebrant is free to choose the weekday Mass, an optional memorial, the Mass of a saint listed in the Martyrology for that day (but not found in the Ordo), Mass for some need or occasion or a votive Mass.[19] In a week when all the days are ferial it is important to introduce some variety. Masses for needs or occasions are chosen according to pastoral exigencies. Certain votive Masses are appropriate for specific weekdays: *Wednesday*, the angels (white vestments); *Thursday*, the Holy Eucharist (white vestments); *Friday*, the Holy Cross (red vestments), the Precious Blood (red vestments), the Sacred Heart (on first Fridays, white vestments); *Saturday*, Common of the Blessed Virgin Mary or from the *Collection of Masses in Honor of the Blessed Virgin* (white vestments). Weekday Mass for the dead (violet or black vestments) may be offered on ferial days, but is to be celebrated "sparingly", as every Mass is offered for the living and the dead.[20]

---

[17] Cf. GIRM, no. 355 a.
[18] Cf. GIRM, no. 355 b.
[19] Cf. GIRM, no. 355 c.
[20] Cf. GIRM, no. 355.

378. When choosing the readings for weekday Mass the celebrant should first respect the continuous two-year cycle of readings for year 1 (years with odd numbers) and year 2 (years with even numbers).[21] In this way the pastor offers his people the riches of the Lectionary. When proper readings are provided for a solemnity or feast that falls on a weekday, these always take precedence over those provided in the two-year cycle.[22] However, on obligatory memorials of saints the proper readings or at least one proper reading are usually provided in the Lectionary. Then the celebrant has some freedom to choose. He should bear in mind what is presented in missals or missalettes used by those who are accustomed to come to weekday Mass.

379. Another pastoral "rule of thumb" may be found useful when choosing the readings. If the homily relates more to the life and virtues of the saint, then the proper readings or other readings selected from the appropriate common of the saint may be more suitable than what happens to appear in the continuous cycle. But the readings provided for all the weekdays during Lent and the last days of Advent (December 17 to 24) always take precedence over any readings provided for the memorials of saints.

Mass Celebrated in Latin

380. Mass celebrated in the language of the Roman Rite should be part of the normal schedule for Sundays and solemnities in all cathedrals and major churches. This is especially appropriate in churches where there is a good choir, that is, to ensure that our precious heritage of chant and polyphonic

---

[21] See appendix 3 for the cycles from 2002 A.D. to 2025 A.D.

[22] Cf. *General Instruction on the Lectionary of Mass*, nos. 82, 83.

music is maintained. One Sunday Mass in Latin is obligatory in all basilicas. The *Missale Romanum* of Pope Paul VI envisages the people taking part fully and actively when Mass is celebrated in Latin. Bilingual booklets should be provided so that the faithful can participate fully and, when possible, sing the Kyrie, Gloria, Credo, etc., in accord with the mind of the Church expressed at the Second Vatican Council.[23] For obvious pastoral reasons, the readings should be in the vernacular, but it may be appropriate to chant the Gospel in Latin at a Solemn Mass, provided the people have access to a translation of the text.

381. The venerable preconciliar rite should also find its place in the liturgical life of the Church by way of a generous application of *Ecclesia Dei adflicta*, that is, in accord with the clear intention of Pope John Paul II. When the faithful request the traditional Latin Mass and the diocesan bishop has given permission, the celebrant with the indult must follow the *Missale Romanum* of Blessed John XXIII (1962). He is to celebrate in Latin, without any blending of ceremonies, postures, texts or readings from the modern rite. However, it would seem reasonable to allow some pastoral latitude for a vernacular Epistle and Gospel, provided these are taken from the 1962 Missal. There should also be provision for a "dialogue Mass", if this would be welcomed.[24] In light of

---

[23] Cf. Vatican Council II, SC, no. 54; CB, no. 40. A useful booklet for the people is *The Mass of Vatican II* (San Francisco: Ignatius Press n.d.). Music for the people is found in the booklet *Jubilate Deo* (1974, revised 1987), and the monks of Solesmes have published the plainsong music of the *Missale Romanum* of Paul VI for the choir and for the celebrant at the altar. Nevertheless, this need not exclude more elaborate polyphonic settings of the Mass, when a skilled choir and musicians are available.

[24] Pastoral discernment is required here, in the face of different views. Some who seek the traditional rite are not interested in dialogue Mass, singing or the ceremonial of High Mass. Others interpret the traditional rite in terms of the richer ideals of the liturgical movement. Moreover, the monastic form of this

maintaining those musical settings of the Mass that may not seem appropriate in the modern rite, solemn sung celebrations of the preconciliar rite should take place from time to time in cathedrals and churches where there are extensive musical resources.

Popular Devotions

382. Parallel to the official liturgical year, other ways of observing sacred time have developed, influenced by popular piety, private revelations and ethnic traditions and customs. While the integrity of the liturgical year must always be respected and maintained, the wise pastor also gives due place to the popular devotions of Christ's faithful, especially where these forms of piety are well established in the life of a community or ethnic group. They are useful opportunities for the deeper catechesis and spiritual formation that many people are seeking today. Devotions may also be "doors" for the return to the sacraments of those who have fallen away. Moreover, because intercessory prayer is a constant feature of popular devotions, those who suffer in body, mind and soul are drawn to them. Here, these "little ones" can find Christ's gentle mercy and loving compassion in the heart of the Church.

Devotions Associated with Specific Months

383. The devotional themes for the months of the year remain an important dimension of popular piety in the lives of many Catholic people. However, the devotional observance of months should never overshadow the liturgical seasons of the Church year or detract from the liturgy of the day.

rite currently used in some abbeys in France in fact incorporates the first simplifications that were authorized immediately after the Second Vatican Council.

384. According to custom or influenced by specific feasts, each month of the year has acquired a specific theme. *January* is the month when we honor the Holy Name of Jesus. Because of the Feast of the Presentation of the Lord, *February* is the month of the Purification of the Blessed Virgin. *March* is the month of Saint Joseph because his solemnity is celebrated on March 19. *April* is the month of the Resurrection because the Easter Season occurs at this time.

385. *The Sunday in the Octave of Easter* has been officially designated by Pope John Paul II as Divine Mercy Sunday. The theme should be included in all Masses. In some places, a special Mass is offered in the afternoon, with the customary prayers of Saint Faustina, eucharistic adoration and a Eucharistic Procession. However the text and readings of the Mass are those provided for the Second Sunday of Easter.

386. *May* is Our Lady's month, hence an appropriate time to choose Masses from the *Collection of Masses of the Blessed Virgin Mary*. Because the solemnities of Ascension, Pentecost, the Holy Trinity and Corpus Christi usually occur in May, the Marian theme could be brought into the liturgy through celebrating and preaching on Mary's spousal relationship with the Holy Spirit, her role in the praying Church, her relationship to the Divine Persons of the Trinity and to the Holy Eucharist. According to local custom, a "May altar" may be set up near the sanctuary or, if necessary, in the sanctuary, but to one side so that it does not overshadow or detract from the altar. Alternatively, the permanent Marian shrine or chapel could be adorned with extra lights and flowers. With the evident revival of Marian devotion in recent years, there has been a return to the "May crowning" ceremony. This may be celebrated within a Mass or para-liturgy and adapted to involve children and their parents. A child usually crowns the image, which may then be carried in procession, to the accompaniment of popular Marian hymns. However, the official rite for permanently crowning an image of Our Lady could be adapted and modified for this celebration; see appendix 9, *Crowning an Image of the Blessed Virgin Mary*.

387. *June* is the month of the Sacred Heart. The liturgical focus is obviously the Solemnity of the Sacred Heart of Jesus. If there is a permanent shrine of the Sacred Heart, extra lamps, candles and flowers would be appropriate during this month, or an image of the Sacred Heart might be placed in some prominent place in or near the sanctuary. This month is also a good time to promote the enthronement of the Sacred Heart in families as a celebration of the presence of Christ's love in the domestic church.

388. *July* is traditionally associated with the Precious Blood of Our Lord. It may be customary to celebrate the votive Mass of the Precious Blood on July 1.[25] Preaching on Christ's merciful work of our Redemption would also seem appropriate in this month. *August* is the month of the Assumption, because of Our Lady's solemnity on August 15. *September* is the month of the Holy Cross, because the Feast of the Triumph of the Cross is celebrated on September 14.

389. *October* is the month of the Holy Rosary, widely marked by the public recitation of the Rosary and the promotion of this greatest Marian devotion. The parish school should be involved in this activity as part of the essential Marian catechesis of children. The Rosary indulgence should be an-

---

[25] Considering the devotion of Blessed John XXIII to the Precious Blood, it seems regrettable that the memorial of the Precious Blood on July 1 was suppressed.

nounced to the faithful.[26] *November* is the month of more
intense prayer for the Holy Souls in purgatory, in the light
of the liturgical celebration of November 2, All Souls Day;
see below nos. 394–402. For obvious reasons *December* is
the month of the Advent of Jesus Christ.

Devotions for a Number of Days

390. The devotional life of the Church is also evident when certain times are set aside for more intense prayer in a parish
or religious community. A *triduum* is three days of public
prayer and devotion in order to emphasize the celebration of
a solemnity or a saint. A triduum may include three Solemn
Masses, eucharistic adoration, preaching or lectures, a parish
mission, popular devotions, a concert of religious music and
additional decoration of the church. However, these three
days should respect the Calendar and never overshadow the
liturgical season.

391. A *novena* is nine days of prayer, derived from the prayer of
Our Lady and the apostles in the cenacle (cf. Acts 1:12–14).
A novena may be made privately or publicly according to a
particular devotion and with a specific intention. The public novena of the Immaculate Conception has already been
noted in the context of Advent. But the term is also used for
a regular weekly devotion observed in some churches, such
as the Mother of Perpetual Help, the Miraculous Medal, the
Infant Jesus of Prague. When a priest or deacon leads this
kind of novena, the devotions should include a sermon and
normally conclude with eucharistic adoration and Benediction. If Mass precedes or follows a novena, the celebrant

---

[26] Those reciting five decades of the Rosary in church, as a family at home, as
a religious community or as a pious fraternity may obtain a plenary indulgence
under the usual conditions (cf. *Enchiridion of Indulgences*, revised edition 1986,
concession 48). Under other circumstances the indulgence is partial.

should not wear the chasuble during the novena devotions. Moreover, the practice of incorporating such devotions into the rite of the Mass is not desirable from either a liturgical or a devotional point of view.

392. The *Forty Hours* devotion consists of two days of solemn exposition of the Blessed Sacrament with appropriate liturgical celebrations. This devotion has not only been maintained in some dioceses but seems to be returning with the steady revival of eucharistic adoration around the world. The annual solemn public adoration of the Eucharist, envisaged in Canon 942, could well take the form of the Forty Hours. A detailed adaptation of the Forty Hours to the modern Roman Rite has already been prepared in the United States.[27]

The Solemnity of All Saints, November 1

393. The culmination of the Season of the Year is the Church's celebration of all the saints: those named in her calendars, canonized or beatified, and the multitude of blessed ones who enjoy the beatific vision in heaven. All Saints Day remains a holy day of obligation in many countries. The liturgical color is white. The Solemn Mass of the day should be timed to meet the needs of the faithful, especially where this solemnity is not a public holiday and when the major Mass would best be celebrated in the evening. The homily might well include reflection on the millions of saints known only to God, including Christians we have known in our own lives. This is also a good opportunity to preach on the "universal call to holiness" proclaimed by the Fathers of the Second Vatican Council.[28] Mass should conclude with the

---

[27] See *Order for the Solemn Exposition of the Holy Eucharist* (Collegeville, Minn.: Liturgical Press, 1993).

[28] Cf. *Lumen Gentium*, no. 40; CCC, nos. 2012–16.

solemn blessing for All Saints. In some cultures the visits of the faithful to the cemetery take place on this day, anticipating All Souls Day, but the public rites for the dead, described below, are not appropriate on All Saints Day.

All Souls, November 2

394. On the Commemoration of All the Faithful Departed the Church gathers in solemn suffrage for the souls in purgatory, and the liturgy should express this clearly. The color of the day is black or violet.[29] If the commemoration falls on a Sunday, it is celebrated on that day and the propers for All Souls replace the Sunday texts.

395. A sense of sobriety and restraint should characterize All Souls Day. Flowers are not placed on or near the main altar, and the organ or other instruments are only used to sustain singing.[30] It also seems preferable to use simpler candlesticks on or around the altar, as in Lent.[31]

396. On this day every priest may celebrate three Requiem Masses: (1) for a specific intention, (2) for all the faithful departed and (3) for the Holy Father's intentions. This privilege was granted by Pope Benedict XV in *Incruentum altaris* (1915) and has never been revoked. However, a celebrant may take a stipend for only one of the Masses. Furthermore, the timing of these Masses should respect the needs and working day of parishioners or the members of a religious community, which would not favor celebrating

---

[29] Wearing white on All Souls Day tends to make the liturgy a repetition of All Saints Day. However white would be appropriate in a culture where it is the color of mourning, for example, in Japan.

[30] Cf. CB, no. 397.

[31] In some places the custom of using unbleached wax candles is maintained, but setting up a false catafalque with a pall and candles is no longer permitted.

the three Masses one right after the other. A priest celebrating privately may choose to offer one Mass after the other, consuming the ablutions, which never break the eucharistic fast. Nevertheless, according to our current understanding of the liturgy, he may prefer to separate the celebrations of Mass across the day, or he may combine two celebrations and celebrate the third later in the day.

397. The celebrant may choose from the three Masses provided in the Roman Missal. According to the options available in the wide range of readings provided in the Lectionary, the homily may well develop: our paschal hope of eternal life; the reality and meaning of purgatory; the propitiatory and impetratory nature of the Eucharistic Sacrifice; and the need to pray for the dead as an act of faith, hope and charity within the Body of Christ.[32] The celebrant should also announce the indulgences granted on this day.[33] In accord with the counsel offered to bishops,[34] pastors should respect good popular customs associated with All Souls Day, such as the visit to the cemetery and the blessing of graves, setting up lights and flowers in the cemetery or in part of the church for the departed and the practices of burial societies or local sodalities dedicated to prayer for the Holy Souls.

398. The breviary recommends the public celebration of Lauds and/or Vespers on All Souls Day.[35] As much as possible of

---

[32] See CCC, nos. 954–58, 988–1019, 1010–14, 1020–21. 1030–32, 1051–55.

[33] The faithful who visit a church or cemetery to pray for the faithful departed, saying the Lord's Prayer and the Creed, may gain a plenary indulgence once only under the usual conditions: sacramental confession, Eucharistic Communion and prayer for the Pope's intentions. Through prayer, this indulgence may be given over to the Holy Souls. *Enchiridion of Indulgences*, revised edition, 1986, concession 67.

[34] Cf. CB, no. 396.

[35] The Office of Readings would also be appropriate as a public celebration on this day.

the hour should be sung, preferably led by cantor(s) and choir. The celebrant wears a black or violet cope and stole over the alb or cassock and surplice. He should be assisted by a deacon or deacons, a lector, two candle bearers, a book bearer and a thurifer.[36] It may be found more convenient to join the celebration of Lauds or Vespers to a Mass, either combining it with the rite of Mass[37] or adding it to the Mass.[38]

The Visit to the Cemetery

399. In some places, it is customary to visit the cemetery to bless the graves of the faithful, even to celebrate Mass there, if this can be carried out with proper dignity and under suitable conditions. The Requiem Mass, Lauds, Vespers or a para-liturgy is followed by the sprinkling and incensing of burial sites. If the Liturgy of the Hours or a para-liturgy is celebrated, the celebrant may wear a black or violet cope and stole, over an alb or cassock and surplice. If the sprinkling and incensing immediately follows Mass, he may replace his chasuble with a cope, after the Prayer after Communion.

400. When this rite follows Mass, after the Prayer after Communion the celebrant gives a brief introduction to the rite. Then, he blesses incense at the chair, and, preceded by the thurifer, the cross and candle bearers, the holy water bearer and book bearer, the M.C. and deacon, he goes in procession to the place of burial while a suitable hymn is sung. Assisted by the deacon, M.C. or a server, he first sprinkles and then incenses the burial sites. If he wears a cope, this may be held back on each side by the deacon, M.C. or servers for

---

[36] For details of the ceremonial of the Liturgy of the Hours, see CMRR, nos. 718–41.

[37] See CMRR, nos. 765–70.

[38] See CMRR, nos. 771–73.

the sake of convenience during the sprinkling and incensations.

401. Having returned to the altar, or the point where the sprinkling began, the celebrant then sings or says "Let us pray" and an appropriate prayer chosen from the *Rite of Funerals*, the book bearer attending as usual.[39] The blessing and dismissal follow. After a Mass, a solemn blessing would seem appropriate, such as that provided in the Roman Missal for Easter Season or nos. I, II, and IV for the Season of the Year. If the rite follows the Liturgy of the Hours or a paraliturgy, the dismissal may well be preceded by a blessing and/or the three familiar versicles and responses for the dead, "Requiem æternam dona eis . . ." (Eternal rest grant unto them), etc.

The Bishop Presides on All Souls Day

402. As at all Masses and celebrations for the dead, the bishop wears the plain miter for Mass and for the visit to the cemetery. He carries the crozier if he is the Ordinary or has been granted the privilege by the Ordinary. The diocesan bishop will give precedence to the sprinkling and incensing of the tombs of his predecessors, whether these are located in the cathedral or elsewhere.

November Offerings

403. In the last week of October and on the Solemnity of All Saints and the Commemoration of All the Faithful Departed, in many places it is customary to collect the November offerings, usually in envelopes provided for this purpose. This practice is regulated by particular law and therefore

---

[39] Based on CB, nos. 398–403.

should be carefully supervised by responsible persons.[40] The pastor should dispose of the excess stipends in such a way that Masses requested can be discharged by any other priest within twelve months.[41]

Christ the King

404. The end of the Season of the Year is marked by the Solemnity of Christ the King, celebrated on the Thirty-Fourth or last Sunday in the Season of the Year. The liturgical color is white. This solemnity provides an occasion to preach on the cosmic, social and personal Kingship of Christ,[42] especially through the rich themes of his Kingdom that are proclaimed in the beautiful Preface of the Mass of the day. In the Southern Hemisphere, this Sunday may be preferred as the occasion for a solemn Eucharistic Procession and adoration, because Corpus Christi falls in the winter.

405. In some regions, First Communion is given to children on this Sunday. The pastor should discern whether parishioners would want to take part in this celebration of the Eucharist or whether it should be timed outside the normal schedule of Masses, which could then justify a moderate adaptation of the liturgy for the children.[43] But the proper texts and readings of Christ the King are always to be used.

---

[40] If the money were to be stolen, the priests of the parish would be morally bound to celebrate some Masses without a stipend, to make up for what was lost.

[41] This is in light of CIC, Canon 953, forbidding a priest to accept more offerings than he can discharge in a year.

[42] Cf. CCC, no. 2105.

[43] See CMRR, nos. 572–92. However, if most of the congregation were adults, the use of one of the Eucharistic Prayers for children would not be justified.

The End of the Church Year

406. In the final week of the year of the Church, the eschatological emphasis of Advent is anticipated. In this spirit, the sequence "Dies Iræ" may be chosen as the office hymn during the weekday celebrations of the Liturgy of the Hours. It is divided into three parts: the verses commence at "Dies Iræ" for the Office of Readings, "Quid sum miser" for Morning Prayer and "Peccatricem" for Vespers.[44] So the cycle of the year of the Church ends, only to begin once more with the First Sunday of Advent. Once again, sacrament and word will sanctify time through the sacred action of the liturgy as God's People continue their pilgrimage towards eternity. In the liturgical year of the Church, time itself has become part of the Incarnation of the eternal Word.

> In celebrating this annual cycle of the mysteries of Christ, Holy Church honors the Blessed Virgin Mary, Mother of God, with a special love. She is inseparably linked with the saving work of her Son. In her the Church admires and exalts the most excellent fruit of redemption, and joyfully contemplates, as in a faultless image, that which she herself desires and hopes wholly to be.
>
> — Second Vatican Council, *Sacrosanctum Concilium*, no. 103.

---

[44] Cf. *Liturgy of the Hours*, Thirty-Fourth Week of Ordinary Time (the Season of the Year), note before Monday of this last week of the Church year.

Appendices

APPENDIX ONE

TABLE OF LITURGICAL DAYS

ACCORDING TO THEIR
ORDER OF PRECEDENCE

From the *General Norms of the Liturgical Year*

I

1. Easter Triduum of the Lord's passion and resurrection.

2. Christmas, Easter, Ascension and Pentecost.
   Sundays of Advent, Lent and the Easter season.
   Ash Wednesday.
   Weekdays of Holy Week from Monday to Thursday inclusive.
   Days within the octave of Easter.

3. Solemnities of the Lord, the Blessed Virgin Mary, and saints listed in the General Calendar.
   All Souls

4. Proper solemnities, namely:
   a. Solemnity of the principal patron of the place, that is, the city or state;
   b. Solemnity of the dedication of a particular church and the anniversary;
   c. Solemnity of the title of a particular church;
   d. Solemnity of the title or of the founder or of the principal patron of a religious order or congregation.

II

5. Feasts of the Lord in the General Calendar.

6. Sundays of the Christmas season and Sundays in Ordinary Time [the Season of the Year].

7. Feasts of the Blessed Virgin Mary and of the saints in the General Calendar.

8. Proper feasts, namely:
   a. Feast of the principal patron of the diocese;
   b. Feast of the anniversary of the dedication of the cathedral;
   c. Feast of the principal patron of a region or province or a country or of a wider territory;
   d. Feast of the title, founder or principal patron of an order or congregation and of a religious province, without prejudice to the directives in no. 4;
   e. Other feasts proper to an individual church;
   f. Other feasts listed in the calendar of a diocese or of a religious order or congregation.

9. Weekdays of Advent from December 17 to December 24 inclusive.
   Days within the octave of Christmas.
   Weekdays of Lent.

III

10. Obligatory memorials in the General Calendar.

11. Proper obligatory memorials, namely:
    a. Memorial of a secondary patron of the place, diocese, region, or province, country or wider territory,

or of an order or congregation and of a religious province;

b. Obligatory memorials listed in the calendar of a diocese, or of an order or congregation.

12. Optional memorials, as described in the instructions indicated for the Mass and office may be observed even on the days in no. 9.

In the same manner, obligatory memorials may be celebrated as optional memorials if they happen to fall on the Lenten weekdays.

13. Weekdays of Advent up to December 16 inclusive.

Weekdays of the Christmas season from January 2 until the Saturday after the Epiphany.

Weekdays of the Easter season from Monday after the octave of Easter until the Saturday before Pentecost inclusive.

Weekdays in Ordinary Time.

If several celebrations fall on the same day, the one that holds the higher rank according to the above table is observed. A solemnity, however, which is impeded by a liturgical day that takes precedence over it should be transferred to the closest day which is not a day listed in nos. 1–8 in the table of precedence, the rule of no. 5 remaining in effect. Other celebrations are omitted that year.

If on the same day vespers of the current office and first vespers of the following day are to be celebrated, the vespers of the day holding the higher rank in the table of liturgical days takes precedence; if both days are of the same rank, vespers of the current day takes precedence.

APPENDIX TWO

TABLE OF MOVABLE FEASTS
FROM A.D. 2002

Year	Ash Wednesday	Easter	Ascension
2002	13 Feb	31 Mar	9 or 12 May
2003	5 Mar	20 Apr	29 May/1 Jun
2004	25 Feb	11 Apr	20 or 23 May
2005	9 Feb	27 Mar	5 or 8 May
2006	1 Mar	16 Apr	25 or 28 May
2007	21 Feb	8 Apr	17 or 20 May
2008	6 Feb	23 Mar	1 or 4 May
2009	25 Feb	12 Apr	21 or 24 May
2010	17 Feb	4 Apr	13 or 16 May
2011	9 Mar	24 Apr	2 or 5 Jun
2012	22 Feb	8 Apr	17 or 20 May
2013	13 Feb	31 Mar	9 or 12 May
2014	5 Mar	20 Apr	29 May/1 Jun
2015	18 Feb	5 Apr	14 or 17 May

The alternative dates for the Ascension and Corpus Christi depend on whether the solemnity is celebrated on a Thursday or on the following Sunday.

Year	Pentecost	Corpus Christi	Advent, 1st Sun
2002	19 May	30 May/2 Jun	1 Dec
2003	8 Jun	19 or 22 Jun	30 Nov
2004	30 May	10 or 13 Jun	28 Nov
2005	15 May	26 or 29 May	27 Nov
2006	4 Jun	13 or 18 Jun	3 Dec
2007	27 May	7 or 10 Jun	2 Dec
2008	11 May	22 or 25 May	30 Nov
2009	31 May	11 or 14 Jun	29 Nov
2010	23 May	3 or 6 Jun	28 Nov
2011	12 Jun	23 or 26 Jun	27 Nov
2012	27 May	7 or 10 Jun	2 Dec
2013	19 May	30 May/2 Jun	1 Dec
2014	8 Jun	19 or 22 Jun	30 Nov
2015	24 May	4 or 7 Jun	29 Nov

APPENDIX THREE

CYCLE OF READINGS
FROM A.D. 2002

Year	Sundays	Weekdays
2002	Year A	Year 2
2003	Year B	Year 1
2004	Year C	Year 2
2005	Year A	Year 1
2006	Year B	Year 2
2007	Year C	Year 1
2008	Year A	Year 2
2009	Year B	Year 1
2010	Year C	Year 2
2011	Year A	Year 1
2012	Year B	Year 2
2013	Year C	Year 1
2014	Year A	Year 2
2015	Year B	Year 1
2016	Year C	Year 2
2017	Year A	Year 1
2018	Year B	Year 2
2019	Year C	Year 1
2020	Year A	Year 2
2021	Year B	Year 1
2022	Year C	Year 2
2023	Year A	Year 1
2024	Year B	Year 2
2025	Year C	Year 1

THE PROCLAMATION OF THE BIRTH OF CHRIST

Approved for Use
in the Dioceses of the United States of America
by the National Conference of Catholic Bishops
and Confirmed by the Apostolic See.

INTRODUCTION

1. The *Roman Martyrology* for Christmas day contains a formal announcement of the birth of Christ in the style of a proclamation. It begins with creation and relates the birth of the Lord to the major events and personages of sacred and secular history. The particular events contained in the proclamation help to situate the birth of Jesus in the context of salvation history.

2. The *Proclamation of the Birth of Christ* may be sung or proclaimed after the greeting and introduction of the Christmas Midnight Mass. The Gloria and opening prayer immediately follow the proclamation.

3. The proclamation may also be sung or proclaimed at the Liturgy of the Hours. If it is used at Morning or Evening Prayer, it follows the introduction of the hour and precedes the hymn. When it is proclaimed during the Office of Readings, it precedes the *Te Deum*.

4. According to circumstances, the proclamation may be sung or recited at the ambo by a deacon, cantor or reader.

5. After the greeting of the Mass, the celebrant or another minister may briefly introduce the Mass and *The Proclamation of the Birth of Christ* which follows, using these or similar words.

Throughout the season of Advent, the Church has reflected on God's promises, so often spoken by the prophets, to send a savior to the people of Israel who would be Emmanuel, that is, God with us. In the fullness of time those promises were fulfilled. With hearts full of joy let us listen to the proclamation of our Savior's birth.

6. The deacon (or other minister) then proclaims the birth of our Lord Jesus Christ.

Today, the twenty-fifth day of December,
unknown ages from the time
    when God created the heavens and the earth and then
    formed man and woman in his own image.

Several thousand years after the flood,
when God made the rainbow shine forth
    as a sign of the covenant.

Twenty-one centuries from the time of Abraham and Sarah;
thirteen centuries after Moses led the people of Israel
    out of Egypt

Eleven hundred years from the time of Ruth and the Judges;
one thousand years from the anointing of David as king;
in the sixty-fifth week according to the prophecy of Daniel.

In the one hundred and ninety-fourth Olympiad;
the seven hundred and fifty-second year from the foundation
    of the city of Rome.

The forty-second year of the reign of Octavian Augustus;
the whole world being at peace,
Jesus Christ, eternal God and Son of the eternal Father,
desiring to sanctify the world by his most merciful coming,
being conceived by the Holy Spirit,
and nine months having passed since his conception,
was born in Bethlehem of Judea of the Virgin Mary.

Today is the nativity of our Lord Jesus Christ
    according to the flesh.

7. The Gloria and opening prayer then follow.

APPENDIX FIVE

THE PROCLAMATION OF THE DATE OF EASTER ON EPIPHANY

Approved for Use
in the Dioceses of the United States of America
by the National Conference of Catholic Bishops
and Confirmed by the Apostolic See.

INTRODUCTION

1. The *Proclamation of the Date of Easter on Epiphany* dates from a time when calendars were not readily available. It was necessary to make known the date of Easter in advance, since many celebrations of the liturgical year depend on its date. The number of Sundays that follow Epiphany, the date of Ash Wednesday, and the number of Sundays that follow Pentecost are all computed in relation to Easter.

2. Although calendars now give the date of Easter and the other feasts in the liturgical year for many years in advance, the Epiphany proclamation still has value. It is a reminder of the centrality of the resurrection of the Lord in the liturgical year and the importance of the great mysteries of faith which are celebrated each year.

3. The proclamation may be sung or proclaimed at the ambo by a deacon, cantor or reader either after the gospel or after the prayer after communion.

4. Each year the proper dates for Holy Thursday, Easter, Ash Wednesday, Ascension, Pentecost, and the First Sunday of Advent must be inserted into the text. These dates are found in the table which is included with the introductory

documents of the *Sacramentary*.[1] The form to be used for announcing each date is: the *date* of *month*, e.g., "the seventh of April."

5. On the solemnity of the Epiphany, after the homily or after the prayer after communion, the deacon or, in his absence, another minister announces the date of Easter and the other feasts of the liturgical year according to the following text.

> Dear brothers and sisters, the glory of the Lord has shone upon us,
> and shall ever be manifest among us, until the day of his return.
> Through the rhythms of times and seasons
> let us celebrate the mysteries of salvation.
>
> Let us recall the year's culmination, the Easter Triduum of the Lord:
> his last supper, his crucifixion, his burial and his rising cele-
> brated between the evening of the (*date*) of (*month*)
> (*date of Holy Thursday*)
> and the evening of the (*date*) of (*month*).
> (*date of Easter Sunday*)
>
> Each Easter—as on each Sunday—
> the Holy Church makes present the great and saving deed
> by which Christ has for ever conquered sin and death.
>
> From Easter are reckoned all the days we keep holy.
> Ash Wednesday, the beginning of Lent, will occur on the *date* of *month*.
> The Ascension of the Lord will be commemorated on the *date* of *month*.
> Pentecost, the joyful conclusion of the season of Easter,
> will be celebrated on the *date* of *month*.
> And this year the First Sunday of Advent will be on the *date* of *month*.

---

[1] That is, *The Roman Missal*. [Holy Thursday's date can be calculated by subtracting three days from the date given for Easter.—ED.]

THE PROCLAMATION OF THE DATE OF EASTER

Likewise the pilgrim Church proclaims the passover of Christ
in the feasts of the holy Mother of God, in the feasts of the
Apostles and Saints,
and in the commemoration of the faithful departed.

To Jesus Christ, who was, who is, and who is to come, Lord
of time and history,
be endless praise, for ever and ever,

R̶. Amen. (Amen. Amen.)

APPENDIX SIX

RECEPTION OF THE HOLY OILS BLESSED AT THE CHRISM MASS

Approved for Use
in the Dioceses of the United States of America
by the National Conference of Catholic Bishops
and Confirmed by the Apostolic See.

INTRODUCTION

1. It is appropriate that the oil of the sick, the oil of catechumens, and the holy chrism, which are blessed by the bishop during the Chrism Mass, be presented to and received by the local parish community.

2. The reception of the holy oils may take place at the Mass of the Lord's Supper on Holy Thursday or on another suitable day after the celebration of the Chrism Mass.

3. The oils should be reserved in a suitable repository in the sanctuary or near the baptismal font.

4. The oils, in suitable vessels, are carried in the procession of the gifts, before the bread and wine, by members of the assembly.

5. The oils are received by the priest and are then placed on a suitably prepared table in the sanctuary or in the repository where they will be reserved.

6. As each of the oils is presented, the following or other words may be used to explain the significance of the particular oil.

7. The people's response may be sung.

Presenter of the Oil of the Sick:
  The oil of the sick.
Priest:
  May the sick who are anointed with this oil experience the compassion of Christ and his saving love, in body, mind and soul.
The people may respond:
  Blessed be God for ever.

Presenter of the Oil of Catechumens:
  The oil of the catechumens.
Priest:
  Through anointing with this oil may our catechumens who are preparing to receive the saving waters of baptism be strengthened by Christ to resist the power of Satan and reject evil in all its forms.
The people may respond:
  Blessed be God for ever.

Presenter of the Holy Chrism:
  The holy Chrism.
Priest:
  Through anointing with this perfumed Chrism may children and adults, who are baptized and confirmed, and priests who are ordained, experience the gracious gift of the Holy Spirit.
The people may respond:
  Blessed be God for ever.

The bread and wine for the eucharist are then received and the Mass continues in the usual way.

APPENDIX SEVEN

TENEBRAE

407. Before the last preconciliar reforms of the Divine Office, Matins and Lauds were celebrated together as an anticipated office (that is, the office of the following day) on three evenings of Holy Week: Wednesday, Holy Thursday and Good Friday. This office was known as "Tenebræ", from the word for "shadow", hence "darkness". Tenebræ was a popular rite not only because of its majestic and evocative music but also because its simple but dramatic ceremonial draws worshippers into the darkness of the Passion of Our Lord and thus prepares them for the light of the Resurrection. In recent years, Tenebræ has been revived in some places, celebrated either according to the traditional rite or adapted to the structure of the postconciliar Liturgy of the Hours. Therefore several options are possible.

408. 1. After the preconciliar reforms of the Office and Sacred Triduum, it was not envisaged that Tenebræ be celebrated in the evening, as an anticipated office. It is never to be celebrated on Holy Thursday after the Mass of the Lord's Supper, during the time of adoration. However, in the postconciliar Roman Rite, "a celebration of the Office of Readings and Lauds" is commended on the mornings of Good Friday and Holy Saturday. This celebration is specifically compared to Tenebræ in the *Circular Letter concerning the Preparation and Celebration of the Easter Feasts*, Congregation for Divine Worship, 1988.[2] These are occasions when the

---

[2] Cf. CLE, no. 40. However, Tenebræ is best celebrated at night.

ceremonies and music from the traditional Tenebræ might appropriately be used to enrich the modern office.

409. 2. Where Tenebræ is celebrated according to the traditional rite, it seems best to plan it for the evening of Good Friday, that is, some time later than the afternoon Liturgy of the Passion. It might be reduced somewhat in length according to pastoral needs. However, because of the musical settings, the traditional Latin office or elements from it should only be sung when competent cantors and choir are available and on condition that they have rehearsed it all thoroughly. The organ is never used at Tenebræ, nor is it played before or after this office.

410. 3. A third possibility would be to plan a formal para-liturgy following the ceremonies of Tenebræ. This might consist of the Palm Sunday Passion broken into separate readings (preferably the Passion that is not set for the annual cycle that year), interspersed with psalms. This would be feasible where there are limited musical resources. If skilled cantors and choir are available, selected sung lessons from the traditional Latin office could be included in such a para-liturgy.

Ceremonial Norms for Tenebræ

411. According to precedence, a bishop, priest or deacon presides at the office. The celebrant and other clergy wear choir dress. Stoles and copes are not worn. An M.C. should assist. One server suffices, to extinguish the candles after the psalms. Another would be needed as book bearer if the modern office is followed. Lectors, in fact cantors, are required to intone the lessons of the traditional office at the ambo or at a bare lectern in the center of a formal choir. There can be nine cantors if the traditional rite is followed literally. However, the choir may intone these lessons according to specific settings. Another person is required to make the customary "strepitus", the loud noise at the end of the rite signifying the earthquake at the death of Our Lord. The strepitus is made in a concealed place, unless the less effective way of making this sound by striking office books on the choir stalls is preferred.

412. The Tenebræ hearse is the main symbol of this office. It is a large standard candelabra, usually made of wood, painted black or a somber color. It is shaped like a raised equilateral triangle, with sockets or spikes for fifteen candles arranged on the upper sides of the triangle. Traditionally these candles are made of unbleached wax.

413. The Tenebræ hearse is set up in the sanctuary in front of the altar, on the Epistle side (that is, to the right of the altar, facing it from the nave); the fifteen candles are lit. Six altar candles are lit, also unbleached according to custom. But in accord with modern practice, no candles should burn on or near the bare altar on Good Friday evening, unless the cross venerated in the afternoon is on or in front of the altar. The processional cross and candles are never used at Tenebræ. In some concealed place, an object is prepared that will make the strepitus (for example, a large wooden hammer and block of wood). A long candle snuffer is placed near the hearse or where the server appointed for this duty sits.

(a) According to the Traditional Rite

414. The traditional rite is described first, because this is the basis for the options of adapting to the modern office or planning a formal para-liturgy.

415. The celebrant, clergy in choir, servers, cantors and/or choir enter in silence and reverence the altar. If the cross for ven-

eration on Good Friday is on or in front of the altar, they
genuflect to it. The celebrant takes the "first place in choir".

416. At the end of the first psalm the M.C. or server takes the
snuffer, bows to the altar, and extinguishes the lowest candle on the left side of the hearse. At the end of the second
psalm the lowest candle on the right side of the hearse is
extinguished, and so on, so that candles are extinguished on
alternating sides after the nine psalms of Matins and the five
psalms at Lauds. This leaves only the candle at the summit
of the hearse burning at the end of the office.

417. The psalms for each Nocturn are chanted by cantors and
choir. The "Gloria Patri . . ." is omitted at the end of each
psalm. At the end of the third psalm for each Nocturn,
the cantors sing the versicle and all respond. All stand as
the Lord's Prayer is recited silently. Escorted by the M.C.,
the lectors/cantors go to the ambo or lectern to chant the
lessons. During each lesson, the M.C. stands on the left of
the lector, who places both hands on the book. No blessings are sought before these readings, and the final "Tu
autem . . ." is omitted. The M.C. and lector reverence the
altar before and after each lesson, and the M.C. escorts the
lector back to his place in choir. However, any or all of the
lessons of the First Nocturn, that is, the Lamentations of
Jeremiah, may be sung by the choir, in which case lectors
do not go to the lectern. The celebrant does not sing the
last lesson, as is customary at other celebrations of the traditional form of Matins.

418. After the ninth responsory Lauds commences. All stand for
the intonation and sit after that of the first psalm. All stand
for the Benedictus. At the sixth verse ("ut sine timore" [free
to worship him without fear]), the server extinguishes the
altar candle farthest to the left, that is, facing the altar from

the nave. He then proceeds to the other side of the altar and extinguishes the corresponding candle; then he goes back and forth, without haste, so that a candle is extinguished during each of the last six verses of the Gospel canticle. Once the six altar candles have been extinguished all lights in the church are put out, leaving only a single candle burning at the summit of the hearse. All sit while the antiphon at the end of the Benedictus is sung. All kneel as soon as "Christus factus est . . ." begins. The Lord's Prayer is said silently. The celebrant says the prayer "Respice . . ." (or the prayer for Holy Saturday) but adds the conclusion silently. By custom the strepitus is made now, then all who have assisted in the sanctuary or in choir reverence the altar as usual and return to the sacristy in silence.

(b) Adapted to the Liturgy of the Hours

419. The Office of Readings and Morning Prayer for Holy Saturday, celebrated in the morning, may be sung accompanied by the traditional Tenebræ ceremonial. However, to maintain the musical tradition, a selection of the intoned lessons and appropriate readings from the traditional Tenebræ should be inserted into the Office of Readings, which may always be expanded for pastoral reasons.

420. The celebrant, clergy in choir, servers, cantors and/or choir enter in silence and reverence the altar. If the cross for veneration on Good Friday is on or in front of the altar, they genuflect to it. The celebrant goes directly to the presidential chair, and the book bearer stands before him as he intones the introduction to the office.

421. In the postconciliar office there are only six psalms for the Office of Readings and Morning Prayer combined, therefore some adaptation of extinguishing the fifteen hearse candles is required. One procedure might be as follows. At the end of the first psalm the M.C. or server takes the snuffer, bows to the altar and extinguishes the two lowest candles on the hearse. At the end of the second psalm the next two candles on each side of the hearse are extinguished, and so on, so that six candles are extinguished after the three psalms of the Office of Readings. Then the next last candle on the left side is extinguished after the first responsory of the Office of Readings and the corresponding candle on the right side is extinguished after the second responsory. Two candles on each side are extinguished after each of the three psalms of Morning Prayer. This leaves only the candle at the summit of the hearse burning at the end of the office.

422. Lectors go to the ambo for the two or more readings of the Office of Readings and the shorter reading of Morning Prayer. Lectors/cantors go to the ambo to chant any Tenebræ lessons that have been chosen to be included in the Office of Readings. The M.C. may stand on the lector's left during these lessons. Any or all of the traditional lessons may be sung by the choir.

423. After the Office of Readings, Morning Prayer commences immediately. Because two hours are combined, the collect at the conclusion of the Office of Readings and the office hymn of Morning Prayer are omitted. All sit during the singing of the psalms and the reading. All may kneel according to custom as soon as "Christ became obedient . . ." begins. All stand for the Benedictus. At the sixth verse ("ut sine timore" [free to worship him without fear]), the server extinguishes the altar candle farthest to the left, that is, facing the altar from the nave. He then proceeds to the other side of the altar and extinguishes the corresponding candle, then he goes back and forth, without haste, so that a candle is extinguished during each of the last six verses of the Gospel canticle. Once the six altar candles have been extinguished,

all lights in the church are put out, leaving only a single candle burning at the summit of the hearse. The intercessions, the Lord's Prayer and collect follow, the book bearer attending the celebrant at the chair. The celebrant gives a simple blessing and dismisses the assembly. By custom the strepitus is made now, then all who have assisted in the sanctuary or in choir reverence the altar as usual and return to the sacristy in silence.

APPENDIX EIGHT
NATIONAL CELEBRATIONS

AUSTRALIA

Ss. Timothy and Titus, feast, transferred to January 23
Australia Day, January 26
St. Patrick, solemnity, March 17
St. Bernadette, optional memorial, April 16
Anzac Day, April 25
St. Mark, feast, transferred to April 26
St. Peter Chanel, memorial, April 28
Our Lady Help of Christians, solemnity, May 24
St. Peter To Rot, optional memorial, July 7
St. Dominic, memorial, transferred to August 5
Bl. Mary MacKillop, feast, August 8
St. Teresa of the child Jesus, feast, October 1
St. Francis Xavier, feast, December 3

CANADA

Bl. André Bessette, optional memorial, January 6
St. Marguerite Bourgeoys, memorial, January 12
St. Bernadette Soubirous, optional memorial, February 18
Bl. Kateri Tekakwitha, optional memorial, April 17
Our Lady of Good Counsel, optional memorial, April 26
Bl. Marie of the Incarnation, optional memorial, April 30
Bl. Marie-Leonie Paradis, optional memorial, May 4
Bl. François de Laval, optional memorial, May 6
Bl. Catherine of Saint Augustine, optional memorial, May 8
St. Eugene de Mazenod, optional memorial, May 21
Bl. Louis-Zepherin Moreau, optional memorial, May 24
Canada Day (Mass for civic occasions), July 1
St. Anne (in the Province of Quebec), memorial, July 26
Bl. Frederic Janssoone, optional memorial, August 5
Bl. Dina Bélanger, memorial, September 4

Ss. Jean de Brébeuf, Isaac Jogues, Antoine Daniel, Gabriel Lalemant, Charles Garnier, Noel Chabanel, René Goupil, and Jean de la Lande, memorial, transferred to September 26
Thanksgiving Day (Mass for civic occasions), second Monday of October
Bl. Marie-Rose Durocher, optional memorial, October 6
St. Marguerite d'Youville, memorial, October 16
Remembrance Day (Mass for civic occasions), November 11
Our Lady of Guadalupe, feast, December 12

ENGLAND

St. David, feast, March 1
St. Patrick, feast, March 17
St. George, feast, April 23
The Beatified Martyrs of England and Wales, feast, May 4
St. George, feast, April 26
St. Bede the Venerable, memorial, May 25
St. Augustine of Canterbury, feast, May 27
St. Alban, memorial, June 20
Ss. John Fisher and Thomas More, feast, June 22
Bl. Dominic of the Mother of God, optional memorial, August 26
St. Gregory the Great, feast, September 3
Our Lady of Ransom, memorial, September 24
St. Edward the Confessor, memorial, October 13
Ss. Cuthbert Mayne, John Houghton, Edmund Campion, Richard Gwynn, and thirty-six companions, feast, October 25
St. Thomas Becket, Feast, December 29

IRELAND

St. Brigid, feast, February 1
St. Patrick, solemnity, March 17
St. Columba, feast, June 9
All Saints of Ireland, feast, November 6
St. Columbanus, feast, November 23

NEW ZEALAND

St. Brigid, optional memorial, February 1
Waitangi Day, February 6
St. Patrick, feast, March 17
St. Bernadette, optional memorial, April 16
Anzac Day, April 25
St. Mark, feast, transferred to April 26
St. Peter Chanel, feast, April 28
Our Lady Help of Christians, memorial, May 24
St. Dominic, memorial, transferred to August 5
Bl. Mary MacKillop, feast, August 8

SCOTLAND

St. Kentigern, memorial, January 13
Bl. John Ogilvie, feast, March 10
St. Patrick, feast, March 17
St. Columba, memorial, June 9
St. Ninian, memorial, August 26
St. Margaret of Scotland, feast, November 16
St. Andrew, solemnity, November 30

SOUTH AFRICA

Bl. Joseph Gerard OMI, Apostle of Lesotho, optional memorial, May 28
Charles Lwanga and Companions, memorial, June 3
Assumption of the Blessed Virgin Mary, solemnity, August 15

UNITED STATES OF AMERICA

St. Elizabeth Ann Seton, memorial, January 4
St. John Neumann, memorial, January 5
Bl. André Bessette, optional memorial, January 6
Bl. Damien Joseph de Veuster of Moloka'i, optional memorial, May 10
St. Isidore the Farmer, optional memorial, May 15

Bl. Junípero Serra, optional memorial, July 1
Independence Day (proper mass for July 4 and other civic observances), July 4
Bl. Kateri Tekakwitha, memorial, July 14
Labor Day (proper Mass for the blessing of human labor), first Monday in September
St. Peter Claver, memorial, September 9
Bl. Marie Rose Durocher, optional memorial, October 6
Ss. Isaac Jogues, John de Brébeuf and Companions, memorial, October 19
St. Frances Xavier Cabrini, memorial, November 13
Thanksgiving Day (proper Mass), fourth Thursday in November
Our Lady of Guadalupe, feast, December 12

WALES

St. David, solemnity, March 1
St. Patrick, feast, March 17
St. George, feast, April 23
The Beatified Martyrs of England and Wales, optional memorial, May 4
Ss. Alban, Julius and Aaron, memorial, June 20
Ss. John Fisher and Thomas More, memorial, June 22
Ss. Cuthbert Mayne, John Houghton, Edmund Campion, Richard Gwynn, and thirty-six companions, feast, October 25

APPENDIX NINE

CROWNING AN IMAGE OF
THE BLESSED VIRGIN MARY

424. The custom of solemnly crowning an image of Our Lady affirms her motherly role as our Queen. Assumed body and soul into heavenly glory, Mary is the great sign and fulfillment of the eternal glory Christ promises to his beloved spouse, the Church. The diocesan bishop should be the celebrant of this symbolic and popular rite that evokes these themes. He may delegate the duty to another bishop or a suitable priest, such as the rector of a Marian sanctuary or the leader or chaplain of a Marian movement. If an image is to be crowned in the name of the Holy Father, the directives in the authorizing papal brief are to be followed. The authorized rite is *The Order of Crowning an Image of the Blessed Virgin Mary*.

425. Out of respect for the Mother of God, the crown is usually fashioned from precious metal and may be adorned with jewels and gems, but it should not be lavish or opulent, especially in a social context where this would cause scandal. Moreover, it should be designed so that its shape, proportions and style are in tasteful harmony with the image. Depending on whether the image is a statue, a painting or a mosaic, it will need to be prepared so that the crown may be conveniently and securely attached to it.

426. The rite of crowning an image of Our Lady is usually celebrated on a Marian solemnity or feast, but never on a solemnity of Our Lord or on a penitential day. The crowning takes place after the homily: at Mass, during Vespers of Our Lady or a Liturgy of the Word. In addition to what is normally required solemn celebration of these rites, the following are to be provided at the credence table or some other convenient place: the crown(s) (usually arranged on a noble cushion), *The Order of Crowning an Image of the Blessed Virgin Mary*, a vessel of holy water and sprinkler. Candles, lamps and flowers should be arranged around or near the image in a way that does not impede the ceremonial.

Crowning during Mass

427. Mass is celebrated as usual up to the homily, which should focus on the readings and the motherly and regal role of the Blessed Mother in the mystery of the Church. After the homily the bishop returns to the cathedra or chair, unless he preached there. He gives the crozier to a server and stands at the cathedra wearing the miter. All stand as the servers bring forward the crown(s). It may be more appropriate for some of the lay faithful to bring the crown(s) to the bishop, for example, leaders of a Marian sodality or a family or some children. The bishop lays aside the miter, and attended by the book bearer, he sings or says the prayer of thanksgiving and invocation, "Blessed are you, Lord", adapting the words depending on whether Our Lady is depicted with her Son or alone. A server brings the vessel of holy water to the deacon, and the bishop sprinkles the crown(s). Then he goes to the image, takes the crown(s) and carefully places it/them on it. If the Blessed Virgin is depicted with her Son, his image is crowned first. If the image cannot be brought onto the sanctuary or is permanently fixed in another place, the bishop may bless the crowns there rather than at the cathedra or in the sanctuary.

428. After the crowning, the antiphon "Mary, Virgin for ever" or some suitable Marian hymn is sung. During the singing, the

thurifer approaches the bishop, incense is prepared with the assistance of the deacon, and the bishop incenses the image. Then he returns to the cathedra or chair. Mass continues with the General Intercessions, as provided in the *Order of Crowning* or in a similar form. After the incensation of the gifts and the altar, the bishop may incense the image once more. At the end of Mass, the bishop then gives the blessing as usual, the deacon dismisses the faithful and the celebration concludes with one of the Marian antiphons ("Salve Regina", "Ave Regina cælorum" or, in the Easter season, "Regina Cæli") or another suitable Marian hymn.

Crowning during Vespers

429. When another liturgical celebration does not take precedence, the crowning takes place during Vespers of the Queenship of Our Lady (August 22) or Vespers of the title of the image. All the preparations are made for solemn pontifical Vespers, with the additional preparations indicated above. At the beginning of Vespers, after the office hymn, the bishop may instruct the faithful on the purpose of the crowning. Then the psalms are sung as usual. A longer reading is appropriate, selected from those provided for feasts of Our Lady in the Lectionary. After the homily, the responsory "Holy Mary Is Queen" or some similar Marian responsory is sung. Then everything proceeds as indicated above, that is, the blessing and sprinkling of the crown(s) and the crowning of the image.

430. After the crowning, the bishop returns to the cathedra, and the Magnificat is sung. The antiphon is taken from the *Order of Crowning*. The bishop prepares incense as usual and goes to the altar. Assisted by the deacon(s), he incenses the altar, the cross and the image. He returns to the chair. The deacon incenses the bishop, the clergy and the faithful. The book bearer attends at the chair for the intercessions, which are taken from the *Order of Crowning*. After the Lord's Prayer the bishop sings or says the prayer "God of mercy" or the collect of the day if this takes precedence. The bishop then gives the blessing as usual, the deacon dismisses the faithful and the celebration concludes with one of the Marian antiphons or another suitable Marian hymn.

Crowning during a Liturgy of the Word

431. All the preparations are made for a celebration of the Word of God, with the additional preparations indicated above. The bishop wears cope and miter and carries the crozier. The entrance hymn is Psalm 45 (44) with the antiphon "The queen stands . . .", or another appropriate Marian hymn. Having kissed the altar the bishop goes to the cathedra or chair, greets the people and gives an appropriate instruction. All stand, and the bishop invites the assembly to pray in silence. He extends his hands and sings or says "O God, since you have given. . . ." He sits, receives the miter, and the readings and psalm follow, selected from those provided for feasts of Our Lady in the Lectionary. The readings for the Queenship of the Blessed Virgin Mary, August 22, are to be preferred. Candles and incense should be used for the proclamation of the Gospel. After the homily everything proceeds as indicated above, that is, the blessing and sprinkling of the crown(s) and the crowning of the image.

432. After the crowning, the bishop returns to the cathedra, where the book bearer attends for the intercessions, which preferably take the form of the beautiful litany from the *Order of Crowning*. The bishop then gives the blessing as usual, the deacon dismisses the faithful and the celebration concludes with one of the Marian antiphons or another suitable Marian hymn.

APPENDIX TEN

DIAGRAM

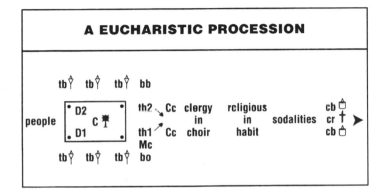

Code for Diagram

C	Celebrant	**cb**	candle bearer
Cc	Concelebrant	**bb**	book bearer
D	Deacon	**th**	thurifer
Mc	Master of Ceremonies	**bo**	boat bearer
cr	cross bearer	**tb**	torch bearer

Bibliography

Primary Sources

Most quotations of Scripture have been taken from the *Revised Standard Version*.

Liturgical Sources

Roman Missal (Sacramentary). *General Instruction of the Roman Missal*. Revised edition, 2000.

The Ceremonial of Bishops. International Commission on English in the Liturgy. Collegeville, Minn.: Liturgical Press, 1989; revised Latin edition, 1995.

Variationes in Libros Liturgicos ad Normam Codicis Iuris Canonici Nuper Promulgati Introducendæ. Typis Polyglottis Vaticanis, 1983.

The I.C.E.L. translations of the rites of the *Roman Ritual* and the *Roman Pontifical* are found in the form of a study edition in *The Rites*. Vol. 1, New York: Pueblo, 1990. Vol. 2, Collegeville, Minn.: Liturgical Press, 1991.

The Roman Ritual, *The Book of Blessings*, International Commission on English in the Liturgy. New York: Catholic Book Publishing Co., 1989.

Liturgical Documents

Vatican Council II, The Conciliar and Postconciliar Documents. Edited by Austin Flannery, O.P. New York: Dominican Publications; Dublin: Costello, 1975.

Vatican Council II, More Postconciliar Documents. Edited by Austin Flannery, O.P. New York: Dominican Publications; Dublin: Costello, 1982.

Official Catholic Teachings, Worship and Liturgy. Edited by James J. McGivern. Wilmington, N.C.: Consortium Books, 1978.

Canon Law

The Code of Canon Law in English translation. London: Collins; Grand Rapids, Mich.: William B. Eerdmans, 1983, 1998.

Secondary Authorities

Duchesne, L. *Christian Worship: Its Origin and Evolution: A Study of the Latin Liturgy up to the Time of Charlemagne*. London: Society for Promoting Christian Knowledge, 1903. A renowned classical resource.

Duffy, Eamon. *The Stripping of the Altars. Traditional Religion in England 1400–1580*. New Haven and London: Yale University Press, 1992. Useful resource for the pre-Reformation background of celebrations.

Elliott, Peter J. *Ceremonies of the Modern Roman Rite: The Eucharist and the Liturgy of the Hours, A Manual for Clergy and All Involved in Liturgical Ministries*. San Francisco: Ignatius Press, 1995.

———. *Liturgical Question Box*. San Francisco: Ignatius Press, 1998. A collection of commonly asked questions most of which appeared in the international missionary magazine *Christ to the World*.

———. *Ministry at the Altar: A Manual for Servers, Acolytes, Clergy, Sacristans, Teachers, Masters of Ceremonies, and all involved in the Ceremonies of the Church*. Sydney: E. J. Dwyer, 1980.

Fortescue, Adrian, and O'Connell, J. B. *The Ceremonies of the Roman Rite Described*. Edited by Scott M. Reid. London: Burns Oates, 1962; London: Saint Austin Press, 1996. This is a fine updated reprint of a classical source for the rubrics of the preconciliar rites.

McDonald, Timothy V. *The Sacristan in the Catholic Church*. Buxhall, Stowmarket, Suffolk: Kevin Mayhew, 1999. This is a compact and well-planned manual for sacristans.

Noonan, James Charles, Jr. *The Church Visible: The Ceremonial Life and Protocol of the Roman Catholic Church*. Viking-Penguin, 1996. This book is full of useful information, with a fearless attention to detail. Some opinions are questionable, and a few points of protocol overlook regional and cultural variants.

Ratzinger, Cardinal Joseph. *The Spirit of the Liturgy*. San Francisco: Ignatius Press, 2000. Whereas texts of the rites and ceremonial manuals present the forms and the externals, Cardinal Ratzinger's masterpiece takes us into the living *faith* that is expressed in the mystery of Christian worship.

Glossary

Antependium: a hanging of fabric or embroidery that may be placed on the altar and/or ambo. The name is from the Latin denoting something that hangs down in front of something else. The antependium is normally of the color of the liturgical day, season or celebration. When used on an altar, it is always placed below or beneath the white altar cloth. It may be draped over the ambo or suspended in front of it. The antependium is also known as an "altar frontal" or a "lectern fall".

Clapper: a device made of two pieces of wood, hinged so as to make a sound when moved vigorously. According to custom, a clapper may replace the sanctus bell at the consecration at the Mass of the Lord's Supper on Holy Thursday, that is, after all bells have fallen silent once they have been rung at the Gloria of that Mass.

Ephphetha: when the celebrant touches the ears and mouth of a newly baptized child, praying that God will open the ears to receive his word and the lips to proclaim the faith, from the Aramaic word used by Jesus Christ, "be opened!" (Mark 7:34). The ephphetha thus recalls the Lord's healing power recorded in the Gospels.

Faldstool: a backless ceremonial chair made of metal or wood. It is used by a bishop or abbot at certain celebrations and may also serve as a *prie-dieu*.

First rite of reconciliation: the celebration of the Sacrament of Penance by personal confession to a priest and individual absolution.

Gremial veil: a veil of silk or linen that is spread on the knees of a bishop or priest to protect his vestments while he is anointing with one of the Holy Oils. It may be white or the same color as the vestments. In practice an amice is often used for this purpose.

Mensa: the upper surface of an altar, from the Latin for "table".

Onomastico: the feast day of the saint whose name a person bears, from the Italian for "name day".

Pricket stand: a candelabra where the faithful light votive candles or lamps before an image or shrine. The term is derived from the old practice of setting candles on a sharp point to secure them.

Rochet: a white garment, similar to a surplice but with narrower sleeves that come to the wrist, like the sleeves of an alb. It is worn as part of choir dress by the Pope, cardinals, archbishops, bishops, abbots, some prelates, canons in some cathedrals and by the chaplains to certain Papal Orders.

Salver: a small tray, usually made of precious metal, on which an object is prepared and presented before or during a ceremony. It is customarily used for the bishop's ring, his skullcap (zucchetto) and the metropolitan archbishop's pallium and its jewelled pins.

Second rite of reconciliation: a communal celebration of the Sacrament of Penance that includes the opportunity for personal confession to a priest and individual absolution.

Strepitus: the loud noise made at the conclusion of the Office of Tenebræ. It represents the sound of the earthquake at the death of Jesus Christ on the cross.

Vimpa: a long veil worn around the neck of the servers who carry the crozier and miter. It covers their hands to protect these objects.

Index

Advent: 25, 42–43, 44 nn.2–3
  as preparation for Christmas,
    47–48
  Sacrament of Penance
    during, 47
  singing carols during, 48
  Sundays in, 44
  weekday Masses in, 379
  wreath, 45
All Saints, November 1: 393
  See also November Offerings
All Souls, November 2: 32,
    394–98
  bishop's celebration of, 402
  visiting cemeteries on, 399–
    401
  See also November Offerings
Anointing of the Sick, Sacra-
    ment of:
  on the World Day of the
    Sick, 87
Annunciation of the Lord,
    March 25: 116
Anthony of Padua, Saint, June
    13: 356
Archangels Michael, Gabriel,
    and Raphael, Feast of.
    See Michael, Gabriel,
    and Raphael, Saints and
    Archangels
Ascension of the Lord: 322–23
Ash Wednesday: 94, 101–3

bishop's celebration of, 104
  immediate preparations for,
    95–100
  preparation of ashes, 94, 105
Assumption of Our Lady: 352

Baptism, Sacrament of:
  conclusion of catechesis
    of newly baptized on
    Pentecost Sunday, 327
  during Easter vigil, 289–93,
    297
Birth of the Blessed Virgin
    Mary, December 8: 358
Blaise, Saint, Bishop and
    Martyr, February 3: 85–86
Blessed Oils and Holy Chrism:
    156, 176 n. 18
  parish reception of, 177–78,
    179 n.20, app.6
  See also Mass of the Chrism

Calendar, Christian:
  catechumenate influences on,
    17
  debate arises over, 12–15
  is established, 18
  roots in Jewish tradition, 9–
    10, 16
  saints' days in the, 19, 33
  Sundays in the, 11
  See also Liturgical Year

The numbers in this index refer to the paragraph numbers in the text rather
than to page numbers.